LEARNING SKILLS SERIES

HOW TO IMPROVE YOUR MEMORY

Robert Leach

nec
NATIONAL
EXTENSION
COLLEGE

Acknowledgements

About the author

Robert Leach has wide experience of developing students' learning skills at all levels from basic to degree level education. He has taught memory courses at South West London and Denman Colleges, and is author of a number of textbooks.

The publishers wish to thank Tim Burton for his invaluable editorial expertise.

The National Extension College (NEC) is an educational trust and is a registered charity with a distinguished body of trustees. Since it was established in 1963, NEC has pioneered the development of flexible learning for adults. NEC is actively developing innovative materials and systems for open and distance learning opportunities on over 150 courses, from basic skills to degree and professional training.

For further details of NEC resources and supported courses, contact:

National Extension College
The Michael Young Centre
Purbeck Road
Cambridge CB2 2HN

Tel: 01223 400200
Fax: 01223 400399
Email: info@nec.ac.uk
Website: www.nec.ac.uk

Registered charity 311454

First published in 1994; reprinted 1995, 2000

ISBN 1 85356 479 6

Contents

	List of techniques	8

Introduction — 9
What this book is about — 9
What this book can do for you — 9
How the book is organised — 9
What this unit is about — 10

Unit 1 — Planning — 11
Learning styles — 13
Reflection — 17
Summary — 17

Unit 2 — Looking at Your Memories — 18
A memory audit — 18
Matching your memory needs with the right units and sections — 20
Strengthening your existing memories — 21
Summary — 25

Unit 3 — Memory Minefields — 26
Research into memory — 26
The power of repetition — 27
The power of circumstances — 28
The forest model — 28
Obstacles to memory — 30
Summary — 34

Unit 4 — Some Basic Techniques — 36
Physical and mental memory aids — 36
SMASHING SCOPE — 38
Summary — 42

Unit 5 — Sounds — 43
Sounds — 43
Spelling and languages — 46
Summary — 49

Unit 6 — Numbers — 51
Funny numbers explained — 52
Number memory systems — 55
Linear and analogue thinking — 58
Summary — 61

Unit 7 — Diagrams and maps — 63
Primacy and recency — 63
Chunking — 63
Routes, maps and diagrams — 69
Summary — 78

Unit 8   **Visions**   **80**
           Visual association   80
           Summary   87

Unit 9   **Review**   **88**
           Name your techniques   88
           Use your techniques   91
           Identify your techniques   92
           Retain your old techniques   92
           Your top ten techniques   93
           Reflection   93
           Summary   94

Appendix   Reading List   **95**

List of techniques used in this book

This list is for quick reference after you have tried the techniques out.

Technique	Page	Aim
1 Backwards chaining	22	
2 Changing points of view	22	to build up memories of past events
3 Picking up on pathways and images	23	
4 Physical memory aids	36	to use diaries, calendars, shopping lists, etc., for forward planning
5 Initial-letter words	39	to remember important words by initials
6 Initial-letter sentences	39	
7 Funny stories	40	to remember a list of people or things by visual memory
8 Repeating names	43	to remember names with the aid of sounds
9 Initial-letter alliteration	44	to remember short lists of concepts
10 Verse and worse	45	to remember a number of words, names, dates
11 Word shapes (right brain)	47	to help with spellings and new words
12 Spotting rules (left brain)	48	
13 Read/copy/hide/write	48	
14 Funny numbers	51	to recall a whole list of words in the right order
15 Sentences for numbers	55	to remember numbers
16 The number-shape peg technique	56	
17 Funny formulae	59	to remember equations and formulae
18 Family trees	66	to remember long lists
19 Numbering pockets	68	to remember where you put things
20 Telescoping	68	to remember classifications
21 Basic shapes	70	to remember maps and diagrams
22 Shorthand signs	72	to remember complex maps and diagrams
23 Spider charts	74	to remember speech and make notes
24 Visual names	82	to remember people's speech with visual memory
25 Memory Palace	82	to remember anything

INTRODUCTION

What this book is about

How to Improve Your Memory will help you to memorise more effectively. The chances are that your memory can be excellent at times. The problem is to recall what you need when you need it.

You will be introduced to a wide range of techniques to improve your memory. The book not only explains these, but also gives you a chance to practise them until they become a part of your normal thinking process. These techniques can help you to remember, at will:

- names and faces;
- numbers and formulae;
- ideas;
- how to do something;
- pictures;
- words and how to spell them;

and much, much more.

What this book can do for you

This book will develop your skills in organising and exploiting your memory, so that your studies, your work and your social life can be richer and more rewarding. The ideas in this book have worked for people in many stages and walks of life. Whether you are at work, at school or college, or enjoying an active retirement, these ideas can make your memories more accessible and help you to memorise new facts and concepts more easily. The suggestions made can be applied to remembering in any context.

If you are a student you will find *How to Improve Your Memory* a particularly valuable aid to your studies. It will help you to apply a range of techniques to remember the concepts and information you need to absorb.

How this book is organised

It is important to understand some of the ways in which the book is put together, so that you can use it to the full. This is not a textbook; it is a book designed to help you to learn for yourself. So a number of special features have been included.

What this unit is about

Each of the units in the book begins with this heading, under which you will find a list of key points to be covered in the unit.

You may not want to work through the whole book from beginning to end. The section entitled *Matching your memory needs with the right units and sections*, on page 20, helps you to match what you need with what the book can provide. For example, if you want to memorise numbers, this matching section will help you to find the units which particularly help in remembering numbers. But you will find that whatever sorts of memory you want to develop, all the techniques may be helpful; so if you have time, work through the rest of the book after you have done first the part that seems most important to you.

Memory techniques

There are twenty-five specific memory techniques explained in the book, and these are listed on page 7. But it is better to work through each unit to gain a good understanding of memory processes, and not just try each technique on its own.

Activity

Although it is possible to get something out of this book by just reading it through, one of the keys to successful memorising involves doing something active. You need actively to process a memory to be confident that it will stick. So the book is full of activities that help you to internalise and develop your memory skills. All activities are indicated by this graphic.

Many of the activities are followed by comments or answers. There may be one right answer, or there may be comments on the range of answers possible. You will probably find it helpful to hide the answers with a piece of card or paper while you do the activity.

Action plan

Throughout the book there are also a number of action plans, which suggest ways of integrating memory techniques into your daily routine.

Self-check

And finally, there are technique summaries which draw together the main points about the detailed techniques.

At the end of each unit, a summary recaps what you have learned. This summary is also a useful aid to memory. The advice often given to people who want to make a successful speech is 'say what you are going to say, then say it, then say what you have said'. As each unit says what it is going to say, then says it, and then recaps, it should help you to remember more successfully.

PLANNING

What this unit is about

In this first unit you will learn how to use this book to improve your memory.

This unit will help you to:

→ review your lifestyle;

→ set yourself a memory goal;

→ determine the learning styles which you prefer;

→ choose the best timings for study periods;

→ maintain mental and physical well-being;

→ understand the two main keys to memorisation – organisation, and strong sensual links.

1 As a first activity, think back to yesterday's news stories. Choose a news item that you might want to remember in future – whether it is a human tragedy, a political event or a sporting triumph.

Now think about how you will go about remembering it. Think of two or three ways in which you will make it stick.

You might have thought of writing the story down, or repeating it to yourself in your head, or visualising the people and places concerned. These are all effective ways to remember. As you work through this book, you will find many others. You will have a wide choice of techniques to choose from. You will also lose that nagging worry that you will forget crucial information just when you need it most.

Reviewing your lifestyle

On a deeper level, if you are concerned generally about your memory, it may be worth stepping back from worries about memory altogether, and examining your general lifestyle.

Suppose, for example, that you are always in such a hurry that you rush to the shops without making a shopping list, and that you curse when you get home because something very obvious is missing. The problem may be to do not with memory, but with stress, disorganisation, or a lack of focus. You need to think of your problem with shopping as part of a general way of life. Perhaps you could change your habits to overcome the difficulty.

On the other hand, perhaps shopping for a specific set of items is really not that important to you. You might prefer to risk missing the occasional replacement bottle of washing-up liquid or cereal packet and spend what would be boring 'shopping-list time' on something else. It is up to you to choose your priorities. So as a first job in your memory improvement course, look at your life in general. Are there any changes that you can make to improve your memory?

2 Write down any changes you can make in your lifestyle to make your memories easier to find when you need them.

There are many possibilities for rethinking and reorganising your life. They can be beneficial generally as well as beneficial for your memory. You could relax more, rethink how you spend your time, consider what unimportant items can be limited or omitted, set priorities for tasks and routines, and give yourself long-term goals. A big goal, such as 'a new job', will give you a good reason for achieving your smaller goals.

Looking at your lifestyle in this way will also help your memory by increasing your:

- relaxation – memories are often blotted out by stress;

- sense of living fully in the present – paradoxically, the more aware you are of your present surroundings, and the more focused you are on what you are doing now, the more accessible relevant memories will be;

- motivation – if you know what your goals are, any memories you need in order to achieve the goals are more likely to be recalled.

Keeping an aim in view

It is important to be clear about what you want to remember, and to set yourself a reasonable goal. Most people's memories have similar general capacities, but you can manage your memory either well or badly. You will be looking at techniques for memory management later in this book. But you need to link these techniques to a learning style and a lifestyle that are comfortable and stimulating for you. To begin this course with a solid goal, think of one aim that you have to achieve. It could be to pass an exam, to act in a play or to prove that you can do something – anything that will require some active memorising.

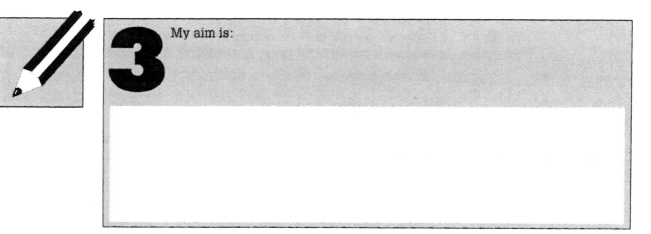

3 My aim is:

Many people are particularly concerned about their memory because they are students, or at least part-time students. If you are not studying, or thinking of studying, skip the next two sections and go on to the section called *Relaxation* on page 15.

Learning styles

Our preferred ways of learning are linked with our preferred memory techniques. When setting out to learn something, some people prefer to listen to a tutor, while others prefer to obtain the same knowledge from a book or video. Some people like to number everything, while others avoid numbers as much as possible. Your memory and your learning skills may improve, however, if you can experiment with various learning styles.

One universal fact about learning is that each of us learns in a very individual way.

Here are some typical learning styles. See which ones most suit you. Tick the box in the *left-hand* column next to each style that you prefer. Then, if you see any new styles you would like to try, tick these in the *right-hand* column.

4 Learning styles questionnaire

	I prefer to	I would like to try to
A MEDIA AND SENSES		
1 Learn using videos, pictures and diagrams	☐	☐
2 Learn with a computer	☐	☐
3 Learn through spoken words – teaching, tapes	☐	☐
4 Learn from textbooks and learning resources	☐	☐
5 Learn through research into documents	☐	☐
B DEPENDENCE AND INDEPENDENCE		
1 Learn by following instructions	☐	☐
2 Learn by problem-solving	☐	☐
3 Learn by negotiating what to study	☐	☐
4 Learn by independent study	☐	☐
C STRUCTURE AND FOCUS		
1 Learn a set syllabus (content)	☐	☐
2 Learn one thing at a time	☐	☐
3 Learn about the course as you go along	☐	☐
4 Learn several things at once	☐	☐
D SELF-RELIANCE AND INTERACTION		
1 Learn on my own	☐	☐
2 Learn with a partner	☐	☐
3 Learn with a small group	☐	☐
4 Learn with a large group	☐	☐

You probably recognise some of these methods, and may want to try others.

The memory techniques in this book are most often applied to the more passive learning styles, for example:

■   learning through teaching and textbooks;

■   learning by following instructions;

■   learning to a set syllabus;

■   learning one thing at a time;

■   learning on your own.

In all these styles the learner is in receptive role, trying to take in a body of knowledge. The other styles are more active and interactive, for example:

■   working with a computer;

■   problem solving;

■   working with several things at once;

■   working with other people.

Each of these styles encourages you to be an active partner in the learning process. These active learning methods have proven advantages in engaging your interest and your memory.

The great advantage of the memory techniques in this book is that they can turn some of the passive types of learning into active ones. You may not be able to negotiate what you learn, or choose your books or tutor, but what you can do is take control of the learning process. With a variety of memory techniques, you can at least choose how you learn, and take an active part in solving the real problems of learning.

While it is unlikely that you will learn, practise and regularly use all twenty-five memory techniques listed in the front of this book, you can experiment with them all, and with different learning styles.

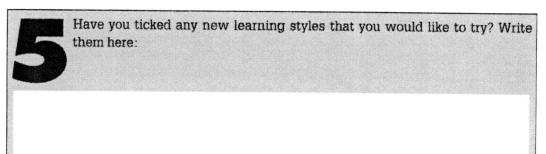

Have you ticked any new learning styles that you would like to try? Write them here:

Try out the new method at the first opportunity. It may be learning with a group, with a video, or by problem-solving; but if it is new to you, and you think it will work, try it.

Timing

If one universal fact about learning is that everyone learns in their own way, another universal fact about learning is that people tend to do it for too long. The problem is not that people spend too many years at school, but that individual periods of study – homework or reading or project sessions – are too long. It is best to study for periods of between 10 and 50 minutes. Make sure that you always take a break from study after a maximum of 50 minutes – and the more intensely you study, the more frequently you should take a break. A short break after study makes all the difference.

Make sure, however, that your breaks come at a natural stage in the material you are studying. And it is best to check through what you have learned just before you break.

It is also advisable that you come back after the break and review immediately the material you just studied before it. This helps you to remember much better. As a visual reminder of this, The Learning Spiral, on page 27, shows you how to pace your study periods.

Note also that it is best to avoid studying at those times of day when you are less alert. Some people are more alert in the morning, some in the evening. After lunch, and late afternoon, tend to be bad times to study.

6 Think ahead to the next time you are going to sit down and study for a long period. Write below your start time and finish time. If your study period is longer than 50 minutes, write also the times when you will take a break within your study session. Make sure you break at an appropriate point, but stick to you timetable as closely as you can.

Start time:
Break from: to:
Finish time:

To encourage yourself to take breaks, even in your most hardworking moments, note that for many kinds of learning, you actually remember better 10 minutes after you finish studying than you do immediately you stop studying. So breaks actually have a beneficial effect on the study, as well as on you.

Positiveness

We all have a tendency to get tense or gloomy when studying, particularly if we are on our own. We need an escape route from cycles of gloom. Everyone has bad periods when they think they can remember nothing and understand nothing, and it is easy to let small things distract us, and to let setbacks depress us.

Change the mood by taking time out. Spend time with other people, enjoy leisure activities, or treat yourself to sweets or a favourite television programme. In the long term, if your study is important to you, your memory won't let you down. You have to help yourself, however, by recognising your weaknesses and allowing yourself adequate relaxation time.

7 What times of day do you study? How often do you take breaks? What do you do when you get tense and depressed? Put your answers here in brief notes.

Relaxation

There is no simple answer to reducing the tensions and stresses of modern life, but the enormous amount of input we receive every day does nothing to help us relax. The capacity to remember is to some extent swamped by the amount of new information we are processing all the time. Quiet reflection, day-dreaming, reliving the past, developing ideas, are all best achieved when you are not also considering new input.

It's a good idea from time to time to switch off – both your own activities, and the television or personal stereo you are listening to – and shut your eyes. Become conscious of the background sounds about you.

8 Shut your eyes for thirty seconds. How many separate sounds can you hear in that time?

You may hear quite a lot, and your brain decides how much to retain of each sound. It uses 20 per cent of the oxygen you consume as it battles to make sense of all the data, even when you are being quiet and receptive. Think how much more complex this process is in a crowded room, with music, people, television, and all the noise and bustle of social life. Many people prefer to study with music or other background noise, while others would find this too distracting. But what we all need is downtime – not furiously enjoying leisure, but enjoying the spaces between activities. These spaces really help us to make sense of our memories, to review them and to integrate them with other memories.

Our physical, muscular tensions also contribute to reducing our ability to remember. Relaxation techniques rely on relaxing the physical state of the body and brain, and can be used as a means to achieve better learning.

One classic relaxation technique involves shutting your eyes and consciously relaxing every part of your body – toes, feet, ankles, legs, body, arms and head – all in great detail and very slowly and deliberately. It can take 10 minutes or more to survey every part of your body mentally and to relax it consciously. The best way is to lie on the floor or a bed. If you have never experienced this, try it. It's well worthwhile.

Whether using this technique or others such as massage, meditation or simply resting, relaxation is an important contributor to a well-tuned memory.

9 How much time can you devote in a week to real physical relaxation? When? Make a note here:

If the answer is none, you may in fact be achieving relaxation in other ways – perhaps through sport or dancing, or even sunbathing. But if you never relax properly, watch out. It's a bad lifestyle for you, and for your memory.

Music

To help you achieve the right relaxed state for good learning, music that has a rhythm that is slightly slower than your heartbeat is very effective. This means that it has to have about sixty beats per minute, or one beat every second. *God Save the Queen* has the right beat, although it might be a little too dramatic to be really relaxing. Try to think of music that you know which is soothing and calm and which has about one beat per second. Songs may distract you with the words, so try to choose instrumental music.

10 Have you got any recorded music that will help you relax? Note its name here:

Calm Purpose

This does not mean going to sleep. In fact, despite some well-publicised methods which claim to teach you by playing tapes while you are asleep, it is now commonly accepted that sleep learning does not work. To learn well, you need to be alert as well as relaxed. Too sleepy, and you learn nothing. Too tense, and the tension blocks your memories.

Reflection

You are now almost at the end of the first unit. You may be surprised that you have not yet practised remembering anything. But you have done a lot of the groundwork necessary before you can improve your memory. You have looked at how the book will work for you, how your state of mind and body helps your memory, how study time should be paced, and how to reflect on your lifestyle and learning styles. You are at the right point to learn the two keys to effective memory techniques. These are:

- organisation;
- strong sensual links.

If you organise your memories, and if you can link them strongly with something or someone you can see, hear, touch, taste or smell, you will develop your memory more and more successfully. The rest of this book will give you many examples of how you can unlock your memories whenever you need them. The next unit begins by looking at ways in which you can match memory techniques to your needs, and make the most of your existing memories.

Summary

In this unit you have:

→ looked at how this book helps you remember;

→ thought about your learning style and lifestyle;

→ thought of relaxation techniques and music;

→ thought about your overall goal;

→ learned the two keys to memory techniques.

Self-check

What are the two keys to memory techniques? (Remember to cover the page above before you note down your answer!)

LOOKING AT YOUR MEMORIES

What this unit is about

In the first half of this unit you will look at the strengths and weaknesses of your memory with the aid of a questionnaire. You can compare your results with those of a recent survey. Then you can select the topics and sections of the book most relevant to your needs.

The second half of the unit introduces you to the three specific memory techniques, which are intended to make the process of reviving memories more effective, whether from childhood or from last night's study.

This unit will help you to:

→ complete a memory audit – assessing your memory;

→ match memory techniques to your needs;

→ strengthen your existing memories.

A Memory Audit

What sort of memory have you got? Are you better at remembering names or dates? Are you absent-minded? How well do you remember appointments and routes? Research has shown that most people who do a memory audit – that is, who fill in a questionnaire like the one below honestly and carefully – give a true, well-balanced picture of their current memory capacities. Try doing this memory audit yourself now.

1	More than once a week	More than once a month	More than once in 6 months	Hardly ever	Never
A Everyday memory					
How often do you:					
1 forget appointments?					
2 lose things at home?					
3 forget to buy something when you go shopping?					
4 have to go back and check that you have done something?					

(continued overleaf)

1	More than once a week	More than once a month	More than once in 6 months	Hardly ever	Never
How often do you:					
5 forget to take with you things that you need?					
6 forget people's names?					
7 forget important numbers (like your phone number, PIN number or car registration)?					
8 forget something you were told yesterday or a few days ago and need to be reminded of it?					
9 try to tell a joke or story but forget the important details?					
10 get lost on a journey you have done before?					
B Study memory					
How often do you:					
11 forget one or more items of a list you have memorised?					
12 forget details of a diagram you have memorised?					
13 find yourself unable to remember the general meaning of an article or lecture, despite taking notes on it?					
14 make mistakes in recalling figures, codes or formulae?					

Take a look at your answers. You are likely to have a good general sense of how your memory works, but you can now check this against the results of your memory audit. You could also ask someone who knows you well to do an audit of your memory independently. If that person gets the same sort of results as you, then you can feel reasonably confident that you know your memory – and its lapses – pretty well.

There is no solid research that indicates what exactly a good memory is. People with busy lives may forget more, but then they have more to remember. However, here are the most typical responses to some of the questions from the 'everyday' section of the above list:

Q2 once in six months,

Q4 more than once in six months,

Q5 more than once in six months,

Q8 more than once in six months,

Q10 hardly ever.

The research on which this list is based, like all the research mentioned, is detailed in the reading list at the back of this book.

Matching your memory needs with the right units and sections

You can follow up your memory audit by matching those areas where you want to improve performance with the relevant sections of the book. In some cases you can match your needs with specific memory techniques, and in others with information sections which help you to understand how your memory works.

1	Appointments	lifestyle (p. 11), all techniques to remember lists.
2	Losing things	family trees and numbered pockets (pp. 66-8), memory palace (p. 82).
3	Forgetting to buy something	lifestyle (p. 11), all techniques to remember lists.
4	Checking back	backward chaining (p. 22), normalisation (p. 33).
5	Taking things with you	family trees and numbered pockets (pp. 66-8), physical aids (p. 36).
6	Names	funny stories (p. 40), repeating names (p. 43), visual names (p. 82), memory palace (p. 82), and all list techniques.
7	Numbers	Unit 6, Numbers, (p. 51) onwards.
8	Forgetting facts you have just been told	lifestyle (p. 11), all techniques.
9	Stories	funny stories (p. 40), funny numbers (p. 51), number-shape peg (p. 56).
10	Routes	Unit 7, diagrams and maps, (pp. 63-79).
11	Lists	Units 4, 5, 6, 7, 8.
12	Diagrams	Unit 7, diagrams and maps, (pp. 63-79).
13	Notes	spider charts (p. 74).
14	Figures	funny formulae (p. 59).

These information sections provide essential knowledge and build up your confidence and motivation to learn the techniques. The numbers on the left of the list above correspond to the questions in the memory audit.

I will be reminding you to review your memory audit when you have completed each unit. That will be a good point at which to think about how the new techniques you learn can help you with the weaknesses you identified. You can also think about particular times when you forgot something, and the ways in which you can avoid such a situation in future.

Strengthening your existing memories

The techniques and suggestions in the units that follow are mainly about learning and recalling new information. To finish this unit, however, we will concentrate on your existing memories, and find ways to bring them to life. These techniques are also a useful back-up to any of the techniques in the rest of the book.

2 Think of your school days. How many names and faces can you remember from your classes when you were 9, when you were 12 and when you were 15?

Write the names here:

Age 9

Age 12

Age 15

Perhaps you remembered a dozen names, perhaps two or three, or perhaps none. Whatever your results, let's now try to activate more memories of that time through a variety of memory-enhancement techniques. These can work for any lost or partly lost memories.

To give you a spur to activate your school-day memories, bear in mind that a recent piece of research encouraged people to remember their schooldays during ten hours of active recalling, using the techniques we will use. At the end, the worst result was that one person remembered eighty-three names of classmates (from their whole school career, not just ages 9 to 15). The best result gave 236 names. These were checked and found to be accurate. The group of people who achieved these feats were a random sample of people aged 22 to 37.

1 Backward chaining[1]

This technique enables you to reach the deep past by going backwards from the present.

- First, think about your recent contacts with old school friends. Have you seen any? Spoken or written to any? Exchanged Christmas cards with any? Write their names on the top line of a piece of paper.

- Then think back to last year and ask yourself the same questions. Write the names you recall on a fresh line.

- Repeat the process for previous years, or groups of years (five-year periods, perhaps, if you are 30 years old now, or decades if you are 60). Write the names of the people on lines going down the page.

- Now you have reached the time when you left school. Who were the people in your class then? Add their names to the list, on another line.

- Go back another year. Write the names of the people in that class, if there were any differences.

- Go back more years until you are back in the class you were in at the age of 13. Add more names to your list as you remember them.

- Go back one more year, to when you were 12. Think back to the people you were with then, and write their names.

- Go back one more year, to when you were 11. Think of the people in your class that year, and write their names. Then go back in the same way to when you were 10 and 9.

You can also 'forward chain' from your first year at school onwards. See if this helps you to add new names to your lists.

3 How many new names have you added by backward and forward chaining? Write the number here:

2 Changing points of view

This technique frees up your memory by reducing the influence of your own remembered feelings of the time. It gives a more objective memory. Your task is to imagine your class when you were aged 11, but not from where you used to sit. Instead, take the place of the teacher. Look along the rows of desks or tables, and see the hard-working, the naughty, the noisy and the quiet children. Think about those who come late and those who forget their homework.

It may seem quite difficult to do this, but do have a go. Don't worry that your imagination will interfere with your memories – as the research results show, your memory will prove quite reliable.

Now take the place of another child, perhaps a friend of yours or another person you remember well. Where did they sit? How did they view the class? What was it like being them? Who did they sit next to, talk to, fight with?

1. All the 26 specific techniques in this book are numbered like this and listed with their page references on page 8. You will be able to review how they work for you in Unit 9.

Shut your eyes for a few minutes to imagine first the teacher's viewpoint, then a child's, then perhaps another child's. If you feel it is useful, you can also imagine yourself as another teacher, or your mother or father. Put yourself in their shoes, and see that world through their eyes.

When you have exhausted your thoughts about your class at age 12, try age 13, 14 and 15. Then go back to when you were 9, and do it again.

4 How many new names have you added by changing your points of view? Write the number here:

3 Picking up on pathways and images

A third technique can be used to bring to light the whole atmosphere of your classroom. You almost certainly have memories which are not of specific people in your class, but of odd details, experiences, places and circumstances which are important to you from that time.

Pathways

It is difficult to bring memories to mind by asking yourself what you were doing twenty-five, ten or five years ago. It is better to ramble quite spontaneously through associations from that time. Your strongest memory might be of your first boyfriend or girlfriend. They might not have been at school with you, but you may remember meeting them at the school gate, or talking about them at school, or even reading a love letter under the desk.

Here are some other possible pathways to connect you with memories of that time.

■ Friendships;
■ brothers and sisters;
■ parents;
■ feelings about Maths, English and other subjects;
■ sports, games, PE;
■ assembly, church, concerts, plays;
■ hobbies, out-of-school groups, outings;
■ tutors.

As you explore memories like these, you may catch a glimpse of members of your class whom you did not remember before. Write down their names, or visualise their faces clearly if the names don't come to mind. Visualise all the faces and conversations – imagine their characteristic behaviour. More names may come back to you.

Images

An alternative but similar technique is to focus on memories of things and places.

Ask yourself the following questions.

■ What did the classroom look like? What was on the wall? What furniture was there? Where was the door?

■ How did the classroom fit into the school? How did I get there from assembly, or after lunch?

■ How did I get to school? On a bus or bicycle, on foot?

■ What were the buildings of the school like? What was around it?

Again, you may find unexpected memories of new people – perhaps getting on the bus with you, or jumping a fence for a short cut to school.

5 How many new names have you added by exploring pathways and images? Write the number here:

6 Now you have tried backward chaining, changing points of view, and exploring pathways and images, you probably have quite a vivid recollection of your school, and you may have remembered more names. If so, write them here:

You may be surprised by how many names you have remembered, or you may be disappointed with the number of new names you found to put here. If so, keep using the ideas above in different ways to trigger your memories. If a direct assault on your memory doesn't produce the goods, a sideways, sneaky approach often does it better.

7 If you need more practice in strengthening existing memories, think back to your childhood holidays. Where did you go on holiday, whom did you go with, and what did you do there? Use the same techniques as with your school memories to bring back your holiday memories.

Action plan: Memory notebook

Now you have made a start on active memorisation techniques, it may be a good idea to start a memory notebook. As the research into classmates showed, you may be able to remember over 280 names of people from school! You can use your memory notebook as a shopping list of things you want to remember, partly lost memories or new items to remember. As you go further through this book, you can note which memory techniques you used for your shopping list of memories. Here is how part of your notebook might look:

Memories	Techniques
My cousins in Canada	backward and forward chaining
The person who borrowed my copy of 'Moonwalker'	picking up on pathways and images

The techniques you have just tried are quite powerful. You can apply them to any context in your past when you want to recall more than that which immediately comes to mind, or when you have tried to remember things by other methods but have failed.

Start your memory notebook by making a list of the memories which you will activate with these techniques.

Summary

In this unit you have:

→ completed a memory audit – assessing your memory;

→ matched your memory needs with relevant pages of this book;

→ strengthened your existing memories by:

backward chaining;

changing points of view;

picking up on pathways and images.

Self-check

As you work through this book, you will have a chance to practise a total of twenty-five memory techniques. When you have done this, you'll have the chance to review which ones work best for you, and for what.

This unit introduced you to the first three techniques. See if you can list these below:

1

2

3

If you are in any doubt, check back to the summary.

Remember to look back at your memory audit before you go on to the next unit.

UNIT
3

MEMORY MINEFIELDS

What this unit is about

This unit is called *Memory minefields* because there are at least two kinds of minefield that you have to negotiate to improve your memory. One is the minefield of misleading ideas about how you remember things. The other is the minefield of the real processes of your memory, which often seem to act against you as much as for you. So the unit is largely a factual one, and is the main location in this book of information about how memory works. The chapter will give you a vital background to encourage your work on specific techniques in the rest of the book.

This unit will help you to:

→ gain an overview of research into memory;

→ understand the role of repetition and of circumstances;

→ visualise the forest model of how the memory works;

→ conquer everyday obstacles to memory.

→ overcomes misleading ideas about memory.

Research into memory

Many thinkers have produced wildly inaccurate and negative ideas about memory. Although our brain cells (neurons) die from birth onwards, in fact we remember more and more as we get older. While the connections between our brain cells are few at birth, by the time we reach old age there are tens of thousands of billions of connections linking neuron to neuron throughout our brains.

For students who worry that they will forget everything after their exam, recent research shows that study memories remain fairly accessible even eleven years after the end of a course, and that these memory levels are likely to remain constant for the rest of your life.

However, the links are only reinforced if we review, rehearse or repeat our memories actively. This was first proved a hundred years ago when the first great memory researcher, Herman Ebbinghaus, memorised a list of nonsense syllables (such as WUJ, CAX or SIF) every day and tested himself later.

The more frequently Ebbinghaus repeated his nonsense syllables to himself after first hearing them, the longer he remembered them. The more repetition, the more memory. If he repeated the words 64 times on day one, he only took seven minutes to relearn them on day two; if he repeated them eight times on day one, he took nearly twenty minutes to relearn them on day two.

But what happened when he relearned them? How long did it take before something was permanently memorised? Ebbinghaus showed that there was a very rapid loss of memory in the first few hours. However, if he reviewed his words after twenty minutes, then again after one hour and eight hours, he would lose little memory of them when he reviewed them one day, five days and thirty-one days later. This classic curve of forgetting has been corroborated by many other researchers.

The power of repetition

So if you want to remember things better, you really do have to put more effort into remembering. There is a clear reward: the more you recall something, the more you'll be able to recall it in future. So, you can only feel confident about remembering someone's name in a year's time if you remind yourself of the name once every day for a week, once every week for a month, and once every month for a year. After this, the chances are that you will be able to recall the name in suitable circumstances for the rest of your life.

1 Look at the learning spiral illustrated below. It shows you the time you can allow to elapse before reviewing something that you want to remember permanently.

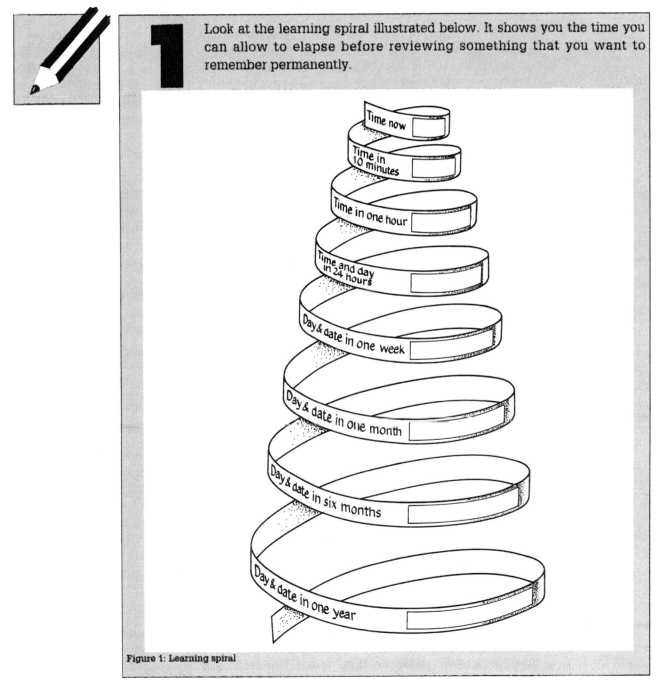

Figure 1: Learning spiral

(continued overleaf)

> Can you think of something that you want to remember all your life? It could be a face, a mathematical formula, or the Latin name of a flower. Whatever it is, memorise it today, and write today's date and the time in the first gap on the spiral. Then write a time ten minutes from now in the next gap. Write tomorrow's date in the next gap, a date a week from now in the next gap and so on.

You may need to note these dates in your diary or on your calendar so that you remember to review your chosen fact at the right intervals. If you do, you should be able to remember it forever.

The power of circumstances

Suitable circumstances act as a powerful motivator for recall. Imagine that fifty years after you last met someone, a mutual friend says to you, 'I've got a surprise for you. I would like you to meet someone you last met fifty years ago'. The chances are that as you see the person's face, his or her name will come unbidden to your tongue. Your brain selects the appropriate memory when it is needed. But if, on the other hand, you have no special reason to recall the name, but you try to make a list of people you knew fifty years ago, you are less likely to be able to call up that particular memory. Your mind may not recognise the urgency or importance of your quest, and your memory may let you down.

What memory training can do is to help you select the categories of things to remember in a way that is desired by the active, conscious mind rather than the less reliable sub-conscious. Memory training allows you to exert control over what you remember, rather than leaving it to chance. The memory techniques you are learning give you this control.

The forest model

Imagine a forest of winter trees. Each has hundreds of branches and twigs reaching upwards and outwards, and hundreds of roots extending downwards and outwards again. Many of the twigs and roots connect with those of their neighbours. Electrical and chemical changes in one tree are passed from it to several neighbours, and then on to several neighbours again until they create complex pathways of change across the whole forest.

Now imagine that the forest is not standing in the soil, but moving – not just walking, like Macbeth's Birnam Wood on its way to Dunsinane, but swimming in soup or even flying. Each tree can move in three dimensions, and can extend or contract its twigs and tiny roots to make and break contact with more and more other trees of the forest. As electrical and chemical messages are passed, the chains of trees constantly reorganise themselves. The frequent messages pass down thick clusters of trees and roots, while an infrequent message may only pass along one thin twig to another twig on its neighbouring tree. The thick clusters don't stay still, however, any more than the twigs which pass only fading messages. Every tree of the forest is constantly changing its position, regrouping with others to make the thick clusters of twigs and roots more and more effective at passing the frequent messages – and thus increasing greatly the chances of those messages getting through to their destination.

This imaginary scene is one way of describing the development of memory, and is based on a model in Steven Rose's book *The Making of Memory*, which won the 1993 Science Book Prize. Each tree in the imaginary forest is a nerve cell or **neuron** in the brain. The trunk of the tree is called an **axon**, and the twigs or tiny roots which contact other neurons are called **synapses**.

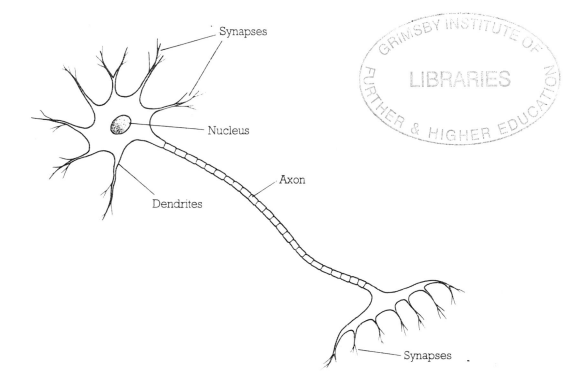

Figure 2: Neuron (brain cell) diagram

The neurons link together in complex ways, just as in our moving 3-D forest. Over a lifetime they will create more and more connections from neuron to neuron until there is an extraordinarily elaborate pattern of connections to represent a lifetime's experience and a lifetime's memories. Sadly, neurons also start dying from the day we are born; so what we gain on the connections we may lose in terms of the overall numbers of neurons. But what is exciting – and important – is that those connections never stop re-organising themselves. There is no such thing as a fossilised brain, or a mechanically stuck brain, or a short-circuited brain. Images of the brain as a clockwork mechanism, or a computer's circuit board, are wide of the mark. The brain is alive, and organic, and constantly in flux.

The brain works hard to achieve all this activity and to overcome damage whenever possible. It uses 25 per cent of all the calories we expend, and uses them fast. We have 20 billion neurons, with up to 100,000 synapses each, making perhaps 100,000 billion links.

Let's pause here for a moment to review the information in this unit so far, and hold the first objective test of your memory of the ideas in this book.

Choose the statement that you think is most accurate from each of the groups below, and put a tick in the corresponding box. Then check your results against the answers at the end of this unit.

From birth onwards:
☐   we start to forget;
☐   we start to remember;
☐   we remember and forget;
☐   we neither remember nor forget until we can focus.

Ebbinghaus found:
☐   that we forget everything if we do not review it;

(continued overleaf)

☐ that we forget 80 per cent of what we learn;

☐ that we can remember 30 per cent of what we learn for 31 days;

☐ that the more often we repeat something, the longer it stays in our memory.

The 'curve of forgetting' shows:

☐ that much memory can become permanent if we review and renew it;

☐ that forgetting accelerates with time;

☐ that we need not try to recall things, as nearly 30 per cent of what we remember will remain permanently;

☐ that it is impossible to remember more than 60 per cent of what we have learned after 20 minutes.

Our brains can be compared most usefully with:

☐ a clockwork mechanism;

☐ a Royal Mail sorting office;

☐ a computer;

☐ a soup full of moving organisms.

During a lifetime, our brains:

☐ become fossilised and slow-moving;

☐ lose most of their power;

☐ build up more and more connections;

☐ decay from birth onwards.

If your answers do not match ours, read back through this section. You may find that the answers become clearer from a second reading. Answering the activity questions, whether rightly or wrongly, will help you to understand the information – but if you do make any mistakes, you must go back to the original information to check your understanding. If you notice anything special about the ideas you missed, this could be an insight into your own memory processes.

Obstacles to memory

Many ideas about memory are completely misleading. It is a good idea to clear these away at the outset. Our own misunderstandings usually originate from famous ideas of the past, so let's review some of the most influential of these.

Great thinkers' misleading ideas

The Graeco-Roman physician, Galen, who was revered as the main authority on medicine until well into the nineteenth century, thought that our memories are kept in our heart and lungs. Other thinkers have suggested more abstract, but equally wrong, concepts which are all too prevalent.

The white board

Tutors can write and draw on a new classroom white board until it is full up. Then they have to wipe it clean and start again. This is a concept of memory as a blank slate which has dominated thinkers for 2000 years. Plato and Cicero in classical times, and Skinner and behaviourist psychologists more recently, have thought of the memory as a blank, wipeable surface on which tutors can 'imprint' messages – but to a limited point only. Once it is full, you have to wipe it clean and start again.

These ideas were quite wrong. Messages aren't 'imprinted' in a permanent place in the memory – they come into the memory and become part of a continuously changing, ever adaptable memory system. Because the system has enormous capacity – around twenty billion neurons – there is never a need to 'wipe' memories. That doesn't mean that all memories are accessible in their original form, but it does mean that they are not destroyed for lack of space.

Just like clockwork?

Another major misleading idea about memory is that it is like a machine. Nowadays the machine is usually a computer, but in the seventeenth century it was a hydraulic machine pumping memories through pipes and turning taps on and off. Between hydraulics and computers came concepts of clocks, industrial machinery and telephone exchanges. Each of these comparisons assumes that our memories can be programmed like industrial robots. We follow fixed routines, and each part of our brains has a fixed function – for instance, to store or combine data, or pass messages. We are considered to be closed systems, black boxes with inputs that make us remember, and outputs that show our memories.

In fact, we are not like that at all. We are human, we think, we forget, we make mistakes, we have marvellous sudden insights, and we can create. If one way won't work, we'll try another way. We are not machines, and if someone throws a spanner in the works we can redesign the works – and even incorporate the spanner in the new design.

The non-existent memory molecule

Many researchers in the 1960s and 1970s thought that they had proved that animals could remember things outside their experience by eating bits of another animal's brain. These gruesome experiments started with flatworms and ended with rats and mice. They were supposed to prove that particular molecules in the brain give memories, and that these molecules can give new memories to an individual who eats them. The research methods were flawed, and the research went out of fashion. It was rather like what nineteenth century phrenologists were doing in allotting different parts of the brain to childhood, emotions, religion, tastes and so on. But it was not helpful.

There is little hard evidence of how memories physically affect our brains, but it is certainly true that there are specific changes in the proteins that form links between neurons when certain types of new experience take place and form memories. The extraordinary thing is that even the smallest new memory appears to affect every single neuron in our brain: not just the left or right brain, not just the temporal lobe, but all of the cerebral cortex and beyond. So our brains are integrated, and our memories are linked in subtle ways across our whole experience.

3 Here is a quick quiz to speed the process of removing unwanted assumptions. Tick 'true' or 'false' alongside each of the following statements. You will find the answers at the end of the unit.

		True	False
1	Memory is located in the heart and lungs.	☐	☐
2	Flatworms can remember by eating other flatworms.	☐	☐

(continued overleaf)

		True	*False*
3	Each memory is in a specific place in your brain.	☐	☐
4	New memories affect every part of your brain.	☐	☐
5	You can't teach an old dog (or person) new tricks.	☐	☐
6	We process experiences as a computer processes data.	☐	☐
7	When your memory is full, you have to lose some memories to take more in.	☐	☐
8	Memory is almost inexhaustible.	☐	☐

Everyday obstacles to memory

Ebbinghaus's research into his memories of meaningless words led to 100 years of laboratory research into memories of other meaningless words, meaningless signs, meaningless pictures and objects and processes. Because researchers liked to be scientific, they needed to research memories that would be of similar value to anyone they tested – and the only way they could do this, was to choose memories of no value. All this research has been called '100 years of silence' by recent researchers into everyday memory, because the period was completely silent about our memories of the real world, our life histories, our studies, our work and social lives. However, more recently a new stream of research has started into 'everyday memory', and a lot of useful information has been gathered which shows how we erect everyday obstacles to memory. Here are some of the commonest.

I saw it with my own eyes

One obstacle to memory is the idea that eyewitness evidence is the best kind. The evidence of eyewitnesses is often treated as conclusive proof of a crime and a criminal's guilt. But we overemphasise our ability to remember the face of a man we saw once only, or to recall stressful and violent events. Indeed we overemphasise the accuracy of our memory generally. We are quite impressionable, so if we believe subsequently that someone is guilty, we may sometimes adjust our memories to suit. We may 'recognise' someone whom we have never seen, or completely fail to remember details of a crime or accident because we are so shocked by it. But with the memory-strengthening techniques of Unit 2, you can do a lot to retrieve accurate and full memories of an event.

'Flashbulb' memories: unforgettable experiences

Most of us have treasured memories from our early childhood, important memories of events at school, memories of meeting lovers, and what are called 'flashbulb' memories – vivid memories of hearing a piece of news, like John Lennon's death or the sinking of the Belgrano, the Argentinian battleship cruiser. Older people often seem to remember their childhood particularly well. Recent research suggests, however, that those treasured childhood or 'flashbulb' memories are only special because we review them often. The experiences themselves are less important than our repeated reviews of them in making them stick in the memory. In fact, research into recent and remote memories shows that, in general, recent memories are much more vivid than remote ones. Childhood memories may seem more vivid to older people because they spend more time reflecting on them. And sometimes they are vivid to us, not because we remember them, but because our parents often repeat them to us. We have childhood photos, too, which may reinforce our memories.

Rose-tinted glasses

Rose-tinted glasses really do exist. People tend to remember pleasant things more readily than they remember unpleasant things. We might try not to focus too much on our unpleasant and neutral memories, in an attempt to make them fade away. It has been suggested that half our memories are pleasant, thirty per cent are unpleasant, and twenty per cent are neutral. In general we tend to romanticise our memories. We might hark back to our first love, our first car, or the days before computers, in a nostalgic way which makes them seem better than they really were.

Normalisation

We tend to remember familiar types of experience as more normal than they really are. Rather than remembering every individual railway station we have seen, we lump them together in our memories as a type of place – and we expect to find platforms, a ticket office, a departure board or monitor, and so on.

This normalisation tendency applies to all our memories, and is both a good and bad thing. It is good because it gives us a general sense of what is normal – of what to expect in a railway station, or what happens at a wedding, or how rabbits jump.

The bad thing about normalisation is that it makes you think that all examples of one type of event, such as a wedding, is much like another. Your sister's wedding cake might be confused in your memory with your friend's wedding cake. Your memory of one wedding is overlaid on another, and the same applies to all experiences that can be put into a 'typical' framework. So although you may only go to one Hindu wedding in your life, the details of it may be more memorable than specific memories of other, more typical British weddings.

Arousal

This is not referring to sexual arousal, but is another psychologist's word to indicate how alert you are. We have a wide range of arousal levels – from very low in deep sleep, to very high in a panic attack. Emotional involvement helps memory, but desperation doesn't. If you want to remember, be wide awake and calm – although not too calm.

4 Working through this activity should enable you to weed out any remaining misunderstandings about how memory works. When you have finished, compare notes with the answers at the end of the unit

		True	False
1	Eye witnesses remember violent crimes well, as the events and people are burned into their memory.	☐	☐
2	Memories never change later because of another person's influence.	☐	☐
3	Most people can work out that they know more than they thought they did.	☐	☐
4	We always remember the bad things that happen to us, not the good.	☐	☐
5	We have unique, special memories of important events and nothing can interfere with them.	☐	☐

(continued overleaf)

	True	False
6 We remember the details of one journey out of a hundred down the same route better than the details of another journey in an unknown area.	☐	☐
7 The calmer and more relaxed you are, the better you remember.	☐	☐

Summary

In this unit we have found out about:

→ research into memory;

→ the power of repetition;

→ the power of circumstances;

→ the forest model of how the memory works;

→ great thinkers' misleading ideas;

→ everyday obstacles to memory.

These fundamental ideas can give you an essential understanding of how and why memory seems to work better in some ways than others. This increased awareness of memory processes will help you to make the best use of the memory techniques in the units that follow.

Action plan

Look back at your memory audit to review your memory problems in the light of the research information outlined above. Does it help you to understand more about how your memory lets you down? Can you think of any practical solutions? If so, write them down in your memory notebook.

Self-check

Can you still remember the names of the memory techniques in the last unit?

1

2

3

Check back to the last unit if – but *only* if – your memory proves hard to retrieve.

Answers

Activity 2

1   (c)

2   (d)

3   (a)

4   (d)

5   (c)

Activity 3

1, 2, 3, 5, 6 and 7 are false

4 and 8 are true

Activity 4

1, 2, 4, 5, 6 and 7 are false

3 is true

SOME BASIC TECHNIQUES

What this unit is about

In this unit, you will have the chance to practise some very useful basic memorising techniques. We will consider how you use aids such as diaries and calendars to help your memory now, and you will go on to learn the principles of effective memorising. You will have a chance to develop skills in making up funny stories using the ideas of SMASHING SCOPE. This unit will also provide case studies of actual memory successes to show how memory aids work.

This unit will help you to:

→ review your physical and mental memory aids;

→ remember the SMASHING SCOPE of memory;

→ use initial letters to remember lists;

→ create funny stories to remember lists.

Physical and mental memory aids

Memorising techniques can be physical, like a diary, or mental, like backwards chaining. Mental memory aids help you remember things entirely 'in your head'. But anyone with a busy life may also rely on physical aids. For instance, you might rely on a knotted handkerchief, or putting your suit near the front door to remind you to get it cleaned. We use these physical aids particularly to remember future events or duties – birthdays, rotas, paying the bills, or whatever – although mental aids can be just as effective for this.

You should take the time to evaluate your use of physical aids before you decide where to put your efforts in developing mental ones. Check your physical memory aids with the list below.

4 Physical memory aids

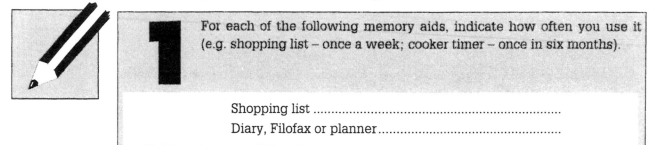

1 For each of the following memory aids, indicate how often you use it (e.g. shopping list – once a week; cooker timer – once in six months).

Shopping list ....

Diary, Filofax or planner..

(continued opposite)

Electronic memory aids (on a desk computer or personal
organiser) ....

Writing on your hand ....

Alarm clock ....

Cooker timer ....

Notes to yourself...

Calendar or wall planner ....

Do you find you use these aids more than once a week? In fact, the more you use them
the better – memory aids of any kind are a sign of an organised approach to
remembering. It is interesting to note that in some research into the use of these aids,
a group of housewives said they used shopping lists and diaries all the time,
calendars about once a week, alarm clocks a bit more often, and the rest hardly at all.
A group of students gave similar results. They used all the physical aids in the same
sort of way, but less often, perhaps reflecting a less structured lifestyle and fewer
responsibilities.

Think about how effective these aids are or can be in solving your memory problems.
Look at the memory audit in Unit 1 to see where physical aids have their place.

You may choose to use physical aids for some of the items in the shopping list of the
memory notebook you started on p. 24.

Mental memory aids

Memory-enhancing techniques have been used since the earliest times. Until reading
and writing were widespread, people regularly remembered long stories, sagas of
ancestors, genealogical tables and much more that we would find daunting today. But
the ideas for managing memories mentally remain the same, although informed and
improved by science.

There are a number of memory specialists who make a living from improving other
people's memories. You see plenty of adverts like the three below, which fairly scream
at you that effortless, miraculous solutions are possible. It is not true. As Ebbinghaus
found, memories are built, not eaten as a flatworm might eat another flatworm. What
memory aids can do is to make your memorising efforts effective.

Figure 3: Adverts for memory methods by Buzan and Fixit

Tony Buzan's techniques are hyped in advertisements, but he has a good line in snappy, memorable phrases. One such is Smashin' Scope. It is a phrase to bring to mind all the ways our memories like to be jogged. We will add a G to it here, to make it SMASHING SCOPE, because G is for goals – and your memory will in general only work for you if you have a goal in mind –if you have a genuine reason to recall a memory.

SMASHING SCOPE

SMASHING SCOPE stands for:

S	sensuality	S	signs
M	movement	C	colours
A	association	O	order
S	sexual interest	P	positiveness
H	humour	E	exaggeration
I	imagination		
N	numbers		
G	goals		

All these qualities help to make things more memorable, and we will use them in the activities and techniques that follow.

Sensuality	Because we need to feel, touch, taste, smell, hear or see objects and people in a full, sensual way to remember them properly. Textures, shapes, scents, sounds and shades affect us strongly.
Movement	Because moving things attract our attention more than still things.
Associations	Because our brains thrive on associations. If we associate strongly an experience with a memory, that experience will always recall that memory. If we associate one strongly memorable thing with a boring but important idea or fact that we need to remember, the memorable thing can lead us to the important idea.
Sexual interest	Because sex is important to us – and you might add children and pets as other strong interests with an emotional tie. When you want to remember a story, a sexual, romantic or cute angle helps it along.
Humour	Because absurd images and ideas are vivid, and pleasant, and so may endure.
Imagination	Because if we imagine a scene, if we put real effort into making a fantasy come alive for us, it has a special quality. We own it, we have built it, and we tend to want to keep it.
Numbers	Because, although numbers are a turn off for many people, counting is a useful way of checking that you have recalled all the items in a particular batch. Numbers are also strong graphic signs, which can be associated in imagination with other things. And they can help you to remember things in the right order.
Goals	Because our minds are very practical. We will remember where our cup is now, because we will need it, but we rarely remember exactly where we put it last week. We remember what we need and want to remember.

Signs	Because they can be shorthand for longer ideas, and tend to be graphic and memorable.
Colours	Because they illuminate, expand, harmonise, contrast, liven up and brighten any memory.
Order	Because it gives a structure to our memories. Order, or sequence, can be a story or a family tree or a numerical or alphabetical order.
Positiveness	Because pleasant memories stick better than ugly ones.
Exaggeration	Because a molehill is more memorable if you think of it as a mountain.

The words that make up SMASHING SCOPE are underpinning ideas for this book, and will always help you to think of ways to improve your memory. They are not a list of alternative methods; sometimes a number of the ideas can be used together. See Funny stories, on page 40, to see how this can be done.

5 Initial-letter words

Of course, the words SMASHING SCOPE are themselves an aid to memorising. The technique of making words like this is helpful because the words give a structure to a set of ideas. For the first word-processing programs, WYSIWYG was the word made from 'what you see is what you get'. WIMP – window, icon, menus, pulldown – denotes features on computer screens

6 Initial-letter sentences

Initial letters can make sentences as well as words:

'Every Good Boy Deserves Favour' gives you the notes on the lines of a musical stave – EGBDF. 'Every Active Dog Gets Bored Easily' gives you the notes to tune a guitar to – EADGBE. 'Richard Of York Gave Battle In Vain' gives you the colours of the rainbow (Red, Orange, Yellow, Green, Blue, Indigo, Violet).

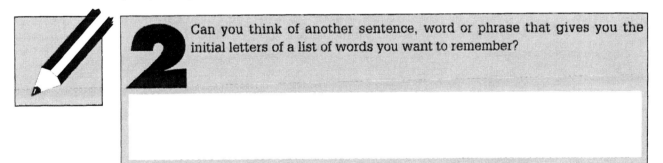

2 Can you think of another sentence, word or phrase that gives you the initial letters of a list of words you want to remember?

3 There is a group of chemical elements called the halides, or Group 7. The group is made up of Fluorine, Chlorine, Bromine and Iodine. Can you write a short phrase to remind yourself of them?

There are many possibilities. You could let your imagination run riot, or stick to something simple like 'Flies Can Bring Illness'.

4 Try the same thing with a longer list – the planets from the Sun to Pluto. They are Mercury, Venus, Earth, Mars, Jupiter, Saturn, Uranus, Neptune, Pluto. Make up a sentence to remember them in the correct order.

Again, all sorts of answers are possible. One boy thought of 'More Valentines Every Month Joyfully Satisfy Universally Needed Popularity', and another surreal contribution was 'My Vineyard Exploded Mysteriously. Jail Stupid Ugly Nasty Pigs.'

5 Now for a surprise check on your memorising. What does SMASHING SCOPE stand for? Note down your answer below, and refer back to page 38 to check it.

7 Funny stories

A very powerful memory technique, which can make use of all the ideas in SMASHING SCOPE, is to involve all the things or people you want to remember in a funny story.

The story can be **S**ensual – full of views, smells, feelings, tastes and sounds. It **M**oves, of course, as all stories must. It creates **A**ssociations between the memorable events of the story and your list of things to remember. It can use **S**ex and **H**umour, and must use **I**magination. **N**umbers can be involved as needed, and your **G**oals are met by the exercise. You can bring in **S**igns – arrows, pound signs or whatever – drench everything you really want to remember in bright **C**olours, create **O**rder by the order of events in the story, be **P**ositive, and **E**xaggerate.

In each of the following two case studies, a memorisation problem has been solved with a funny story.

Case study 1: Nineteen people's names

I had to spend a weekend with nineteen new people, and wanted them to have confidence in my ability to get to know them, appreciate them and remember them. I had a list of their names, and they were listed according to the area they came from. I thought at first that I might be able to remember the areas, and then the people from each area, but there were twelve areas – too many to make it worth remembering them. So I wrote the list of nineteen names out alphabetically, and tried to think of a way to remember them. I thought of SMASHING SCOPE, and came up with a silly love story. This is how it went. The people's real names are in bold, and the words they reminded me of are in italics.

(continued opposite)

Big **Aldan Allen** was a muscly blackbearded **Carter** from smelly **Coe Comfort Fern** (*Cold Comfort Farm*). He was a **Godman**, but he had **Hirons** (*his eye on*) a red-haired **Hooker** who was **Hughes** (*huge*) and came from the rosy thatched cottages of **Hutchcroft Hutcheson Hutchings**. He couldn't disguise his feelings and said '**Oliver!**' (*I love her*) '**Parfitt**' (*perfect*), she said. 'Oh,' he panted, you make me '**Phipps**' (*untranslatable*). Then she dragged him through the brambles to a clearing on a **Thornhill**. They were made for each other. They got married, and prospered, and moved to a **Whitehall** to rear their **Young**.

When I'd remembered the story, I knew all the names. Hutchcroft Hutcheson Hutchings could have been rabbit hutches, I suppose, but it was a funny and memorable combination of names anyway. When the time came for our weekend, I stood up in front of everyone and said their names without notes. They were quite impressed.

Later on, as you will see in Unit 8, the names were also linked to faces.

Case study 2: Shopping list

I hadn't brought pen or paper to the campsite, but there were a number of things I had to get from town, and as I'd have to cycle a long way, I wanted to make sure I'd remember them all. Tent pegs, tomatoes, a can opener, dental floss, margarine, a sharp knife, toothpaste and a tea towel. They didn't fit into categories very well, so I made up a story about them. I made the objects have a kind of wheelbarrow race, where the long things were wheelbarrows and the other things pushed them. I had the tomatoes pushing the tent pegs, the margarine pushing the can opener, the dental floss – unravelled but stiff – pushed by the toothpaste (although it could have been the other way round), and the knife pushed by the tea towel. It was unlikely, but it was memorable.

Now it's your turn to make up a story.

Think of some things you have to remember. (Use your memory notebook and audit to help you if necessary.)

- When you have made your choice, think about the items you have selected, and allow SMASHING SCOPE to inspire you to bring them to life in a story.
- When you have created your story, think it through a few times in your head; then write it down for the record.

The process of making up a story can sometimes come easily, and sometimes not. It depends on all sorts of things – the original list, your own imagination and mood, your experience of story telling, your experience with SMASHING SCOPE, and much more. You may be interested later to see how you have developed your memory skills, so take time now to make plans for another occasion when you can make up a story to remember something. The following technique summary will help you with your planning.

Technique summary: Funny stories

The *Technique summaries* in this book are designed for general use, now or in the future. You can save them up for the next opportunity, or work through them straightaway.

1 List the facts to be remembered.

2 Think of all the ideas in SMASHING SCOPE one by one. How can they help?

3 If you make up a story, who will be the main characters?

4 How can you bring in all the items you want to remember?

5 How can you make them all memorable in the story?

Think about these stages when creating your next funny story, and put it together when you are ready.

Summary

That brings you to the end of Unit 4. You have now:

➔ reviewed your physical and mental memory aids;

➔ memorised the SMASHING SCOPE of memory;

➔ used initial-letter words and initial-letter sentences to remember lists;

➔ created funny stories to remember lists.

Self-check

It is time again to check your memory of the names of the memory techniques so far.

Below is a jumbled list of the words that make up the names of the first six memory techniques. See if you can you put them back together in the right order.

pathways and images	backwards	points of view	picking up on
chaining	physical	stories	initial letter	funny
sentences	words	changing	initial letter	memory aids

Check back through Units 2 and 4 if you want to recap on the techniques.

Answers

Self-check

1 Backwards chaining.

2 Changing points of view.

3 Picking up on pathways and images.

4 Physical memory aids.

5 Initial-letter words.

6 Initial-letter sentences.

7 Funny stories.

SOUNDS

What this unit is about

This unit will allow you to practise saying and writing names, rhymes and other memorable words. You will see how sounds, and other techniques, can help you to spell words.

This unit will help you to:

→ learn how sounds can help you remember;

→ use sounds for spelling and learning languages.

Sounds

Sounds can be a great memory aid. Because sounds are alive and vivid, and ring in your ears, they have the necessary qualities to make a strong sensual link to your memories.

Researchers have described a short-term memory process which can only hold a few sounds at a time (about six syllables in English, or nine in faster-spoken Chinese). To get sounds into a longer-term memory, help is needed. Repeating words aloud is an excellent memory aid. You hear the sounds, feel the movement of your tongue and breath, sense the rhythm of the words. Whether it is your lover's name or the eight-times table, it reinforces the sounds and the sense of the sounds, creating a multiple echo from sound to meaning and back again. The only thing that stands in the way of vastly increasing your memory by this technique is the possible embarrassment at muttering in the presence of others. Overcome the embarrassment, and you can learn to remember far more.

8 Repeating names

People's names are also a source of embarrassment. How do you remember them when you haven't got a list? One simple answer, used by many television presenters, is to repeat a person's name as soon as you are introduced. It may seem a little forced at first, but you soon realise the benefits.

1 Here is most of an imaginary conversation. Fill in the missing part, using the other people's names as often as you can.

(continued overleaf)

Albert:	This is Sue. Sue's new to the club.
You:	
Sue:	Hello! It's nice to meet you and Albert. Have you been members for long?
You:	
Albert:	And I've been a member for eight years.
Sue:	Well, I obviously have a lot to learn from you!
Albert:	Oh, I wouldn't say that, she'll soon pick it up, won't she?
You:	
Sue:	Thanks!

You could find at least three chances to use Sue's name, and perhaps Albert's as well. Each time you repeat the names, you will remember them better. It will also help if later that day you review all the new people you have met and repeat their names aloud as you visualise their faces. Repeating names is a sure way to remember them, and can even increase your popularity.

As this technique can help you remember names, so it can help with any new words or numbers you have to learn. The more chances you have to repeat them aloud, the better.

9 Initial-letter alliteration

Alliteration is the term used to describe repetition of the same sounds. For example: 'In Hertford, Hereford, and Hampshire, hurricanes hardly ever happen', or 'lady of the lowlands'.

In studying marketing, as with many other subjects, alliteration helps considerably. Important concepts are made memorable by shared initial letters. There are the Three Ps (Product, Place and Price), and – for more advanced learners – Promotion, Publicity, and Positioning. Other examples include communicating with the Five Cs – be concise, clear, courteous, complete and correct. A management guru tells companies to be the Four F's – fast, friendly, flexible, and fun.

2 These techniques, like all the others in this book, are most likely to take root if you link them with your own experience.

Can you make use of any group of words (like Product, Place, Price), which relies on alliteration to be memorable? Write it below:

If you remembered them rapidly, the alliteration may have helped your memory.

10 Verse and worse

Historians in particular appear to have been attracted by alliteration, humour, rhythm and rhyme. Perhaps they are emulating Julius Caesar, who wrote 'veni, vidi, vici' (I came, I saw, I conquered) when he had defeated the Gauls. You probably know 'Remember remember the fifth of November' and 'In fourteen-hundred-and-ninety-two, Columbus sailed the ocean blue'.

The following example of another historical rhyme tells you the Queens and Kings of England.

> Willy, Willy, Harry, Steve,
>
> Harry, Dick, John, Harry three,
>
> Teds three, Dick, Harries four to six,
>
> Teds four, five, Dick, Harries twix,
>
> Mary, Liz, Ted, Jaz, Chaz, Olly,
>
> Chaz, Jaz, Willy (Mary's folly),
>
> Anna, Georges one to four,
>
> Will, Vic, Ted, George, Ted outdoors,
>
> George the six and Lizzy two,
>
> What are Chaz and Di to do?

This gives you the names of forty-one monarchs (including Oliver Cromwell) with extra comments on the love life of William and Mary and Charles and Diana, and on the abdication of Edward VIII. It's an economical and effective skeleton for traditional English history.

3 Recent presidents of the United States include Clinton, Bush, Reagan, Carter, Ford, Nixon and Johnson.

Try to make up a rhyme to remember their names. Aim for memorability, not literary merit!

You could have tried something like the following.

> Johnson's not so bad as Nixon
>
> Ford and Carter better than Reagan
>
> But Bush is even worse than Clinton.

(Although this would depend on your political and historical approach!)

These rhymes have no artistic value but they can help you to memorise awkward facts, especially if you make up the rhymes yourself.

4 Think of some terms or names you want to remember, and turn them into a rhyme.

Look out for songs that you can adapt to fit the words you need to remember. For example Elvis Presley's 'Love me Tender' could go with the chemical elements we listed:

'Love me Fluorine, love me Chlorine, Bromine dreams fulfil; Oh my darling Iodine you, and I always will.'

Keep practising your versifying skills when you want to remember boring facts. The verse helps the words to come alive, the sound echoes in your ear, and the rhythm and rhyme help to make a sensual link to the driest abstract ideas.

Technique summary

1 List the words you have to remember.

2 Find a rhythm for them.

3 Find an existing song or a new verse.

4 Squeeze them to fit, with some memorable nonsense involved.

Remember to use this technique summary whenever you need to try out this technique for your own requirements.

Spelling and Languages

Repeating aloud can help you to remember spellings, but due to the quaint spelling system of the English language repeating the sounds alone will not be enough for spelling. You can also call on other methods, as you will see in Activity 5. But first, a little more information.

Left and right brains

The left and right lobes of our brains are not independent. They work together in an integrated way for tasks like reading and spelling, but, as the diagram opposite shows, the left and right lobes do each have different functions. There seems to be a tendency for spelling out a word (e.g. 'p—a—r—l—i—a—m—e—n-t') to be a function of the left of the brain, while seeing a word as a whole (parliament) may be part of the right brain's function. Thus the sound-based approach to spelling and reading, in which syllables are learnt separately, is a left brain method, while the 'whole word' approach, is a function of the right brain. To learn to spell, or to learn foreign vocabulary, it is useful to draw on both sides of the brain.

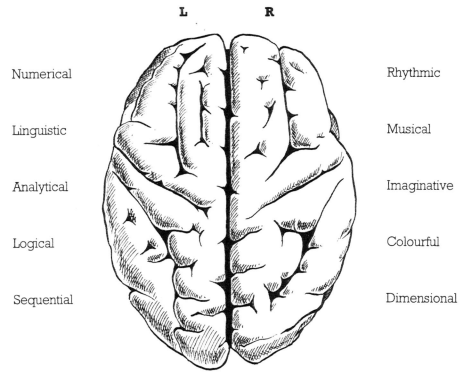

L   R

Numerical   Rhythmic

Linguistic   Musical

Analytical   Imaginative

Logical   Colourful

Sequential   Dimensional

Figure 4: Lobes of the brain

Spelling system

prophesy	prophecy			
glycerine	mandarin			
tambourine	humorous	coloration		
heinous	inveigle			
accede	secede	supersede	exceed	succeed
subtly	treacly	accoutring	manoeuvring	

Look at the following list of words that many people find difficult to spell:

These words are in pairs and groups of contrasting spellings. For Activity 5 (on page 48) you will choose a few words, in pairs or groups, which include a word you cannot always spell correctly.

11 Word shapes (right brain)

It can be helpful to visualise the shapes of words and imagine pictures that remind you of the spellings of those words. For example, 'tambourine' has 'ou' in the middle, while 'humorous' and 'coloration' have 'o' alone. You can imagine that the 'u' in tambourine' is a hand holding the 'o', which is a tambourine, and shaking it to make sounds. The 'o' of humorous, on the other hand, could be a laughing mouth on its own, and the 'o' of coloration could be a 360° rainbow on its own.

You can also visualise with other words. 'Prophesy' is a verb – an action – and the 'sy' sounds like 'sigh' (and many prophets may seem to sigh when they prophesy). 'Prophecy', on the other hand, is a noun – a thing.

12 Spotting rules (left brain)

The other way to remember how to spell involves the left brain, which covers logic and rules. In prophesy and prophecy, the verb, the action, has 's', while the noun, the thing, has 'c'. The same rule applies with other pairs of words, as in the following examples.

Verb	Noun
Advise	Advice
Devise	Device
Practise	Practice

Your left brain can probably uncover many other rules that can help you with spelling; but in English there are a lot of awkward words where neither the left brain nor the right brain approach is particularly helpful. However, you can still memorise the differences in sounds. Advise sounds like ad**vize**, while advice sounds like ad**vice**; and prophesy sighs while prophecy sees.

13 Read-copy-hide-write

When you have done your best to remember a word or spelling using the techniques described so far, you often still need to settle down to the old but tried technique of read–copy–hide–write. This is a classic way to remember spellings, and works as follows.

First, do what you can by using the visualisation technique, and applying any rules that may be appropriate. Then read the words aloud several times before copying them out.

After this, hide the words (using the piece of card that you use to hide activity answers) and write them again. Check you did it correctly. Wait ten minutes, and write the words again. If you got them wrong this time, look and read aloud and copy them again. If you got them right, do the same thing a day and week later. Each time you make a mistake, go back to the beginning and start again.

5 Now copy out the words you have chosen from the list on page 47:

Note any visualisation you can imagine (word or picture):

Note any spelling rules which apply:

(continued opposite)

Read the words aloud several times.
Hide the words, and then write them here:

Do the same thing after ten minutes here:

After a day, write the words again here:

Technique summary

1   Identify words which you always forget how to spell.

2   Write them in a notebook or computer file.

3   Visualise, spot rules and say the words aloud.

4   Read, copy, hide and write as many times as necessary.

Summary

In this unit you have learned:

→   how sounds can help you remember;

→   how to use sounds for spelling.

Self-check

1   Try looking back at your memory audit in Unit 2, and see how you are getting on in sorting out some ideas to improve your memory.

2   Can you remember the names of the memory techniques so far? List them below:

Unit 2

1 Backward ....

2 Changing ....

3 Picking up on ....

Unit 4

4 Physical ....

5 .... letter words

6 .... sentences

7 .... stories

Unit 5

8 Repeating ....

9 Initial .... alliteration

10 .... and worse

11 Word .... (right brain)

12 Spotting .... (left brain)

13 Read/copy/hide/ ....

14 ....

Action plan

Check back with your memory audit, then look at your memory notebook and add any techniques or items to remember that you feel are useful or important. You will have the chance to review all the techniques when you reach the end of this book.

NUMBERS

What this unit is about

This unit introduces some humorous techniques which will enable you to remember numbers.

The unit starts with a technique known as *Funny numbers*, which helps you to remember a series of things in the right order and enables you to check that all the items are there.

To remember specific numbers, you can use *Sentences for numbers*, and to remember any number at all, the *Number-shape peg* technique is excellent.

Finally, you will have the chance to try out a technique for remembering formulae in *Funny formulae*, which is of particular use for studying mathematics and physics.

This unit will help you to:

→   use funny numbers to remember lists;

→   use words to remember numbers;

→   use the number-shape peg technique to remember numbers;

→   remember numbers and formulae.

14 Funny numbers

This is a remarkably useful memory technique. Like all the techniques in this book, it has been tried and tested over and over again, but unlike other more complex systems, it is also relatively easy to learn and quickly pays its own rewards. Students of law, business studies, chemistry and many other subjects have benefited from it, and so will you if you try it out seriously.

As SMASHING SCOPE tells us, humour and number are among the best memory aids. By the way, can you remember the words in SMASHING SCOPE? They give you the principles of memorisation.

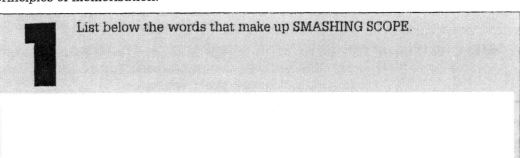

1   List below the words that make up SMASHING SCOPE.

Check back to page 38 if you have missed any of the words.

Funny numbers explained

Humour and number sound like opposites, but they can soon work together with a bit of imagination (that's another SMASHING SCOPE word). This is precisely what the funny numbers technique involves. You need to:

■ think of a list, say six or ten items, although twenty is not too difficult after practice;

■ connect the numbers with images that suggest the item you are numbering.

The fact that you are using numbers means that you can count to make sure that you have remembered everything, and in the correct order where appropriate.

If you can make the links between the numbers and the images funny, they are more memorable. In fact, it is hard to make a list of anything linked with numbers without humour creeping in.

For example, imagine that you are starting to study Environmental Science (a mixture of Biology and Geography with an ecological slant). The six areas within the A-level syllabus are:

■ the physical environment;

■ the living environment;

■ ecology;

■ resources;

■ industrialisation;

■ managing the environment.

So, you number them one to six:

1   the physical environment;

2   the living environment;

3   ecology;

4   resources;

5   industrialisation;

6   managing the environment,

and then have to think of funny images:

1   number one could be a very physical weightlifter with the world on his dumbbells;

2   the living environment could be a number two emerging from an egg, which could also be a globe;

3   number three could be two semicircular arrows linking the soil to plants and to animals, indicating ecological balance;

4   number four could be four strong farm horses, (res-horses = resources) straining to pull the world across a ploughed field;

5   number five could be a semicircular railway track with a huge locomotive or factory steaming away;

6   and six could be a tiny St George, trying to tame a gigantic dragon that swirls round him in the shape of a number six.

Figure 5: **Funny numbers for areas of Environmental Science**

The illustration shows these funny numbers for Environmental Science. See the case study below for how one student used 'funny numbers' for business law.

Case study 3: Funny numbers and law courts

In my first year studying accountancy there was a terrible paper on business law. We had to memorise hundreds of laws and cases and it was real hard work. One question that always came up was on the courts' structure in England and Wales. The right answer would earn an easy few marks, so I used funny numbers.

(continued overleaf)

There are eight courts in the civil system – at least the way I memorised it. These are: the County Court, the High Court – with three Divisions: Queens Bench, Family and Chancery – the Court of Appeal, the House of Lords, and the European Court.

First, I numbered them one to eight, and thought of the County Court as Counting, with a big number one as the big hand counting the minutes on a clock. Two was the High Court, so I made the number two into a really high mountain with clouds floating around it. (I could have done Twin Peaks instead, I suppose.) Then Queens Bench Division was three, so I imagined a bench with three legs and a Queen's Crown on it. Family Division was four, and I imagined a number four with little faces and arms waving about on all the ends of the lines making up the figure four. Chancery Division was five, and I took Chance to be represented by a die showing a five. Court of Appeal was six. I thought of orange peel which had been cut off the orange in one long strip, and twisted to look like a six. The House of Lords was seven. I just put a long judge's wig on a number 7, looking a bit like a bloodhound. Then European Court was eight. I put all the stars of the European Community flag into the shape of an eight.

When I had done all this, I remembered the funny numbers every so often and then, when it came to the exam, I wrote all the courts down without pausing at all.

2 Think of a list of six to twelve items that you want to remember. If you cannot think of any more lists just now, you might try to use funny numbers for one of the lists below.

Criminal Courts	Bones of the skull	Early successful Disney films
Juvenile Court	Parietal	Snow White
Tribunal	Coronal suture	Pinocchio
Magistrates Court	Frontal	Fantasia
Crown Court	Sphenoid	Dumbo
Court of Appeal	Temporal	Bambi
High Court	Zygoma	Cinderella
House of Lords	Mastoid process	101 Dalmatians
European Court	Mandible	Alice
	Mental foramen	Peter Pan
		The Lady and the Tramp
		Sleeping Beauty

Although the Disney list is longest, it should be the easiest to memorise, because there are strong visual images to associate with each number. The medical terms are the most difficult to link to visual imagination – mental foramen might remind you of a maniac supervisor, but you'll have to use your ingenuity. In any case, it is much better if you choose your own list. Remember the G of SMASHING SCOPE stands for goals – your goals and not ours.

(continued opposite)

When you have made your list come alive with funny numbers, think of it for a few minutes, preferably with your eyes shut. When you are sure that all the items are clear in your mind, and in order – from one to six, ten or whatever – then write them down here without copying from an original list.

Number memory systems

15 Sentences for numbers

Numbers are usually harder to remember than words because they often have negative or no associations.

The value of pi (π) – the constant that gives you the circumference of a circle with $2\pi r$ – is impossible to remember absolutely, as it is an 'irrational number' with decimal places that go on forever. School textbooks use 22/7 or 3.14 or 3.142. Mathematicians often need far more than three decimal places, however, and one ingenious way to find the first twenty decimals is given by the following rhyme. The number of letters in each word is equivalent to each number after the decimal point.

I wish I could determine pi	141592
Eureka! cried the great inventor	65358
Christmas pudding Christmas pie	9793
Is the problem's very centre	23846

So, the value of π to 20 decimals is 3.14159265358979323846.

A similar, if shorter, sentence gives the value of $1/\pi$ to six decimal places, as follows:

Now I remember the reciprocal = 0.318310 (reciprocal = 10)

You could use similar ideas to remember numbers that are important to you. If there is a zero, you may have to use a punctuation mark for it. If your number is all high digits, like 889.798, it is unlikely that you will find a sentence to fit.

Find a sentence to remember a phone number. For example: 316644 = Now I wander lonely, half-born.

16 The number-shape peg technique

The number-shape peg technique is the name given to pictures and sentences that can act as mental 'pegs' on which to hang specific combinations of numbers. The numbers that you have to remember are all played by actors in the shape of funny people, funny birds or crocodiles. It is an excellent way to remember long and random numbers with an entertaining series of dramas.

The mysterious parentage of the egg that stands for zero can be the focus of many stories, as you will see. The associations are:

1 a policeman;

2 a swan;

3 a woman with long curly hair;

4 an ostrich;

5 a crocodile standing on its tail;

6 a fat man;

7 a toucan;

8 a fat woman;

9 an elephant;

0 an egg;

(decimal point) a daisy.

Figure 6: Number-shape pictures

See if you can guess the following famous numbers.

1) A policeman carries an egg to two fat men.

2) A policeman rides an ostrich to an elephant riding a swan.

3) A toucan throws an ostrich to another toucan.

You'll find the answers at the end of the unit.

This technique can also be used for more complex numbers, as in the following examples.

- The Stock Exchange stood today at 2912.4.

  A swan on an elephant's back told a policeman to get off another swan, which was pursued by an amorous ostrich with a daisy in its beak.

- An ounce is a small fraction of a kilogram. To be exact 1 oz = 0.02835 kg.

  An egg stood next to a daisy, which was next to another egg. A swan was very proud of them, but a woman and a fat woman were trying to keep a crocodile away.

- The diameter of the sun is 1,392,000 km.

  A policeman, and a woman on the back of an elephant which is spraying water over a swan with three eggs.

2912.4

Figure 7: The Stock Exchange stood today at 2912.4

5 Try making your own number-shape stories using these characters: the egg (0), the policeman (1), the swan (2), the woman (3), the ostrich (4), the crocodile (5), the fat man (6), the toucan (7), the fat woman (8), the elephant (9) and, if needed, the daisy (decimal point). See if you can make stories for these two numbers:

1   2350 x 1800 x 450 mm = the dimensions of a king-sized bed;

2   16,838,885 km = the land area of Russia in 1990. (For this one, you could dress the people up in traditional Russian clothes to remind you what your story means.)

Here are some suggested answers. Compare them with yours and see if yours are as memorable.

1 A swan and a girl run away from a crocodile coming out of an egg in an 'X' shaped trestle cradle. Behind them, a policeman and a fat woman guard two other eggs, one in another 'X' trestle. Behind them, an ostrich fights a crocodile over the ownership of a fourth egg.

2 A policeman is arresting a fat man, while a thin woman is being attacked on both sides by two fat women, and two other fat women are trying to catch a crocodile.

These stories are helpful for various reasons.

- They bring SMASHING SCOPE to numbers, which usually have few memorable features.

- Your efforts in creating the stories are processing the numbers in your mind, embedding them deeply.

- You are turning the randomness of numbers into something which is meaningful to your whole brain – a story about people, birds and animals – rather than series of numbers which may only make sense to your logical left brain.

Linear and analogue thinking

Linear thinking is digital, like a series of instructions (on–off–on–on–off). It follows instructions one by one, and creates order out of chaos. Holistic, right-brain thinking is analogue. It accepts and recognises meaningless patterns, creates and discards them.

It used to be thought that laboratory rats learned about routes through mazes by programming themselves digitally and linearly. That is, they would think: 'take the first right, second left, first left, third right, go straight on, press the lever and this will lead to dinner'. In fact, the rats learned the overall shape of the maze, and could not be confused for long by changes in the pattern of tunnels. They may not have the same right- and left-brain functions as human beings but, like us, they use all the methods available to solve problems. Linear thinking is one way, but analogue thinking, which is based on a spatial approach – patterns, not a single line – is very powerful.

That is why our next unit will concentrate on visual, spatial systems, to make your right brain all the more involved in memorising.

Make a list of six numbers you need to remember. For example, you might note your phone number, bank or building society or credit card account number, PIN number, passport number and national insurance number. Write them below, or on a separate sheet of paper for security.

Make the numbers into stories using the number-shape system. You can remember which number is which by adding features to the story that link in to the meaning of the number. Perhaps you might include flying abroad on a swan for your passport number story.

When you have memorised your stories, you should be much more confident about these important numbers and you will be able to throw away the piece of paper you wrote them on.

17 | **Funny formulae**

This technique is mainly of interest to people who want to learn mathematical formulae.

Now that you have tried making sentences to denote numbers, you may have realised that in Mathematics and Science, few numbers are only numbers. They are values which are combined in expressions such as equations, functions and formulae. The techniques we have looked at so far are not going to help you to remember operators such as addition, subtraction, multiplication, division, let alone signs denoting square roots, brackets and fractions.

You will need new images to remind yourself of these operators, and also for variables like x, y, a or b in algebra.

The examples below are taken from Physics, but the ideas apply to any subject that is related to maths. If you look at these three equations of motion you will see that there are few numbers as such, but plenty of letters and operators.

1   $s = ut + 1/2at^2$

2   $v = u + at$

3   $v^2 = u^2 + 2as$

where s is the distance or displacement, a the acceleration, t the time, u the initial velocity and v the velocity of the object after moving distance s in time t.

Images for variables and operators

The variables in these equations may be people or large objects. For example, let us say:

s =   a sailor;

u =   an undertaker;

a =   an apple (for Newton's discovery of gravity's accelerative power);

t =   a round clock;

v =   a viking.

The operators could be indicated by small adaptations to these images. A shoe could be used to represent the figure 2 as it rhymes. For example:

u^2 =   an undertaker with a shoe on his head;

t^2 =   a clock with a shoe on top;

v^2 =   a viking with a shoe on his helmet.

Equals signs could perhaps be the swords of duellists, held horizontally at a dangerous point in the duel. Multiplication could involve being tied up in ropes making an X around the tied bodies. Addition could be a knotted cord between the elements to be added. Subtraction could be a knife held by the relevant party. Division can be indicated by the dividend sitting on top of the divisor.

So you can now visualise these equations as sword fights between sailors, undertakers and vikings, hampered by various encumbrances.

You might include in your images the people and birds from the number-shape system, or you might develop your own images to help you remember mathematical formulae. Gain some practice at this technique by doing Activity 7, which asks you to devise and use your own characters.

Figure 8: Equations as sword fights

7 Write or draw a visualisation of $e = mc^2$ (Einstein's famous relativity equation), where e is the amount of energy in the universe, m is the mass of the universe, and c is a constant number.

Summary

In this unit you have:

→   used words to remember numbers;

→   remembered numbers and formulae;

→   used funny numbers to remember lists;

→   used peg systems to remember numbers.

Self-check

1   Can you remember the funny story you made up in Unit 4? Write a note of the list you were remembering with your funny numbers.

2   Can you remember the names of the memory techniques so far? List them here:

Unit 2

1   B ....

2   C ....

3   P ....

Unit 4

4   P ....

5   I .... words

6   I .... sentences

7   F ....

Unit 5

8   R ....

9   I .... eration

10   V ....

11   Word .... (............................ brain)

12   Spotting ....(............................ brain)

13   Read/c ....

Unit 6

14   Funny ....

15   Sentences for ....

16   Number-s .... p .... system

17   Funny ....

If there is one you can't remember, look back to the techniques in Unit 2 to help you recall any of the others. Then look back to the list at the front of the book to check your answers.

Action plan

Think about the techniques in this unit. Do they offer any help to your memorisation requirements? Do they remind you of things you need to remember? Note down in your memory notebook techniques and items to remember for future action.

Answers

Activity 4

1   1066

2   1492

3   747

DIAGRAMS AND MAPS

What this unit is about

This unit introduces a number of techniques for remembering lists of items by breaking them down in various ways.

You will practise making long lists manageable by using the *Family tree* technique, and integrating them into systems with the *Telescoping* technique.

Visual versions of the same ideas are developed with *Basic shapes*, a technique which will help you remember diagrams and maps, and *Shorthand signs*, a technique which makes complex maps and diagrams easier to remember and draw. Finally, *Spider charts* are practised to make and remember notes for speeches and other purposes.

This unit will help you to:

➜ organise your memories into snapshot-size family groups;

➜ use family trees to make memories within memories;

➜ see how the same ideas help you remember diagrams;

➜ draw spider charts to help you remember ideas.

Primacy and recency

If you see a series of photographs and then are asked to choose the same selection of photographs from a much bigger collection, the chances are you will do very well. Probably, you can recognise faces and places very easily after one view. However, the images you do forget are likely to be those which are less memorable because they occur in the middle of the series of photographs. It's easier to remember the first few and the last few.

This aspect of memory applies to all kinds of memorisation, and is known as 'primacy' (for our tendency to remember the earliest items in a series), and 'recency' (for our tendency to remember the most recent items). Let us look at how the tendency to forget middle items in a long list can be countered.

Chunking

Dividing a long list into several chunks will help you to avoid forgetting the middle items. A group of seven, plus or minus two, is the best size of group for memorising – and this applies to words, numbers, images, ideas, or anything else.

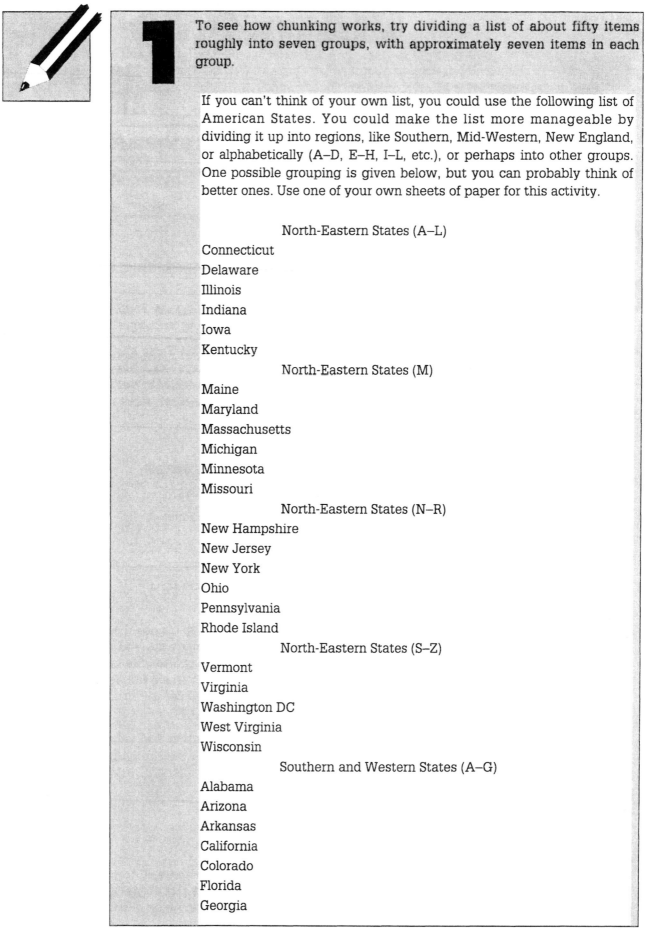

To see how chunking works, try dividing a list of about fifty items roughly into seven groups, with approximately seven items in each group.

If you can't think of your own list, you could use the following list of American States. You could make the list more manageable by dividing it up into regions, like Southern, Mid-Western, New England, or alphabetically (A–D, E–H, I–L, etc.), or perhaps into other groups. One possible grouping is given below, but you can probably think of better ones. Use one of your own sheets of paper for this activity.

North-Eastern States (A–L)
Connecticut
Delaware
Illinois
Indiana
Iowa
Kentucky

North-Eastern States (M)
Maine
Maryland
Massachusetts
Michigan
Minnesota
Missouri

North-Eastern States (N–R)
New Hampshire
New Jersey
New York
Ohio
Pennsylvania
Rhode Island

North-Eastern States (S–Z)
Vermont
Virginia
Washington DC
West Virginia
Wisconsin

Southern and Western States (A–G)
Alabama
Arizona
Arkansas
California
Colorado
Florida
Georgia

(continued opposite)

Southern and Western States (H–M)

Hawaii

Idaho

Kansas

Louisiana

Mississippi

Montana

Southern and Western States (N–O)

Nebraska

Nevada

New Mexico

North Carolina

North Dakota

Oklahoma

Oregon

Southern and Western States (S–Z)

South Carolina

South Dakota

Tennessee

Texas

Utah

Washington

Wyoming

You probably noticed that the list of American States is in eight uneven groups, with rather odd regional and alphabetical divisions. Your groupings should be more logical if possible, but should also be in groups of about seven items in each list. If they are longer, the middle items in each list will be harder to remember.

When you have grouped your list of fifty items, read the list through several times, hide the list, and then try to write down all the items from memory.

How did you do on writing down your lists from memory? Perhaps not brilliantly, but without any other memory aid than chunking, you should have been able to do a lot better than if you had tried to write the fifty items down in random order.

The idea of chunking has been called 'the rule of seven plus or minus two' because this is the best size for a chunk. Chunking is a very important idea behind memorisation skills. If you can chunk or organise your memories into groups of about seven words, phrases, ideas, people or things, then you are already beginning to remember better. This is partly because in the act of grouping you are processing the information on a deep level. You are, for instance, thinking about relevant categories, choosing from your store of categories, perhaps rejecting some, and making decisions based on all your available information, ideas and ways of organising. So you are embedding the new information among the categories in your brain.

Chunking also works partly because each chunk is, quite simply, the right size. It fits the size of our short-term memories.

18 Family Trees

When you have divided your list of fifty into about seven groups, you should make a list of the groups. This is like going back up a family tree from the last generation to the generation before. The list is a further aid to your memory, as each of the items in your list of groups can act as a trigger for recalling the things in that particular group.

For example, you can use this technique to make a shopping list. All the goods are listed for the first shop. For the second shop, the writer has used the family tree technique and found it sufficient to list just the groups. The result is quicker shopping.

Tesco			Texas			
Fruit	**Vegetables**	**Tins**	**Paint**	**Electric**	**Plumbing**	**Wood**
oranges	lettuce	tomatoes				
apples	onion	baked beans				
bananas	cauliflower	spaghetti hoops				
lemons	carrots	corn				
melon	broccoli	tuna				
pears						
Frozen	**Dairy**					
peas	Kraft slices					
fish fingers	Brie					
ice cream	butter					
chicken	fruit					
pizzas	yoghurt					
turkey steaks	greek yoghurt					
	Flora					

3 Try drawing a family tree of two or three generations. It could be of your own family, the Royal family, or perhaps not a family at all, but a classification of types of play, computers or chemical elements, for instance. You don't need any further guidance: the process of deciding how to draw out your 'family tree', and how to link the parts, will make the end result more memorable.

This method of laying out information as a family tree – whether it is a real family, or a different set of lists – is known as a tree diagram, a classification, or a taxonomy. The family tree technique is an excellent way to break up long lists into short lists which are meaningfully related, and can be more easily remembered.

Technique summary

If you have to remember more than six to ten items, primacy and recency tend to make you forget the middle items. This technique helps to overcome this problem.

1 Divide the list into groups of seven (plus or minus two).

2 Give the groups names.

3 Make a list of the groups (and if the list is longer than seven groups, make a list of groups of groups).

4 Memorise the members of each group.

5 Memorise the names of the groups.

4 Now try chunking a new list. Select a list of up to fifty items that you wish to remember. They could be plants for your garden, pop bands you want to keep track of, or new technical terms in your specialist area – new computer models, for example. Don't list all the items here, but list the categories or groups you will divide them into.

Initially, any list may seem unmanageable if you can't count the items on your fingers. But you'll soon become confident in breaking up lists into groups and labelling them to make them accessible.

First, though, let's see how the general principle of chunking, and the family tree technique, can help solve an everyday problem of remembering a list of things and, at the same time, remembering where they are.

Pockets and handbags

5 Make a list below of all the things you usually carry round with you when you go out.

Your list is probably quite a long one, although you will have been able to compile it easily. But do you always remember to take with you everything you have listed? It would be boring to have to go through the whole list every time you go out. It's better if you can chunk the items, either by the place you usually put them or by some characteristic of the items themselves.

19 Numbering pockets

One professor was constantly niggled because he never remembered which pocket he had put things in. Tony Buzan advised him to number his pockets, and always remember the number of the pocket in which he was keeping his ticket, notebook or whatever. The professor's life changed for the better overnight because, from then on, he always put his train ticket in pocket two, his wallet in pocket three, and his handkerchief in pocket four.

Using the list you made in the previous activity, now chunk all the items you included into short lists, with approximately seven items in each list. The chunks can refer to the pocket or part of your bag where you keep the items, or you could use some of the following categories:

- cards;
- keys;
- coins;
- paper money;
- tickets;
- addresses and phone numbers;
- tissues and medical;
- pens and paper;
- tools (comb, tweezers, knife);
- make-up;
- money records (e.g. receipts, credit-card slips);
- miscellaneous.

You have now turned your chunks into a family tree, because you have got a label or 'parent' for each chunk. If you can remember your labels or categories (which might not be a type of item, but just a pocket you keep something in), you are well on the way to remembering everything you've got to carry round with you. These short lists are a lot more manageable than the long lists. If you can remember all the categories, you should be able to check that you have what you need much more quickly whenever you go out, and also that you remember what you've got with you.

Furthermore, if you're ambitious about remembering where things are, try doing the same thing for the drawers and cupboards in your home, or the storage areas in your workplace. If you manage to keep track of possessions in this way, you will save a lot of time searching for things (although you may find you begin to provide a non-stop information service to your family and colleagues!).

20 Telescoping

'Telescoping' is a way of keeping track of items at any level of detail by organising them into groups, then into groups of groups, and then into groups of groups of groups. As long as each group has about seven items, you should be able to do this indefinitely. Just as a telescope can study groups of galaxies, or groups of stars, or groups of planets, or groups of satellites, so you can learn to memorise whole systems – whether biological classification systems, schools of philosophy, or types of widget.

7 Can you think of a system which you would like to memorise? Anything from the names of the teams and the first team players in the Premier League, to varieties of tulip. Name your system here:

What are the names of the groups of items in your system? (If the system is not already divided into manageable groups – of about seven – you will have to divide the groups accordingly.)

You may have a choice of ways to divide up your groups. As long as one way makes sense to you, stick with it.

Try to keep looking out for chances to chunk the things you have to remember into short lists, and telescope the lists into lists of lists. This process helps your thinking as well as your memory, as you have to decide on the best way to classify everything, and this helps you to retain the links more clearly.

Routes, Maps and Diagrams

You can use a variant of the family tree and telescoping approaches to remember routes, maps and diagrams. Let's look at a route-finding technique first.

A useful way to find your way back to your starting point when you visit a place for the first time was pointed out by Gillian Cohen (author of two of the books in the reading list on page 95). The route back will look completely unlike the route out, because you will be seeing the buildings and other features of the landscape from the opposite point of view. Suppose you are going with a friend from the railway station to her house, but have to go back alone. Every time you turn a corner on the way to the friend's house, look behind you to see the buildings from the point of view of someone coming from the opposite direction, and remember which way you came. If you take a visual note of every turning, you can organise your recollections into a series of linked chunks and find your way back to the station easily.

Action plan

Make a note to follow this technique next time you visit a strange area. See how easily you can get back to your starting point without a map.

Now let's turn to techniques for remembering maps and diagrams.

21 **Basic shapes**

To build up an outline map of the world, you can first sketch five triangles for the main continents, excluding Europe. Then use your knowledge of the countries of each continent to build up rough shapes of the land masses (see the illustrations below). You can then refine it further for a better, more accurate rendering.

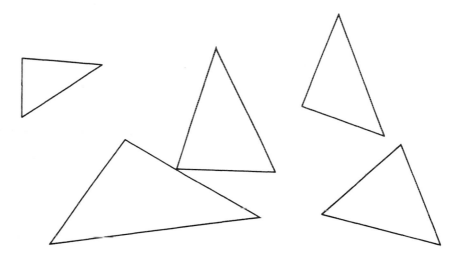

Figure 9.1: A sketch of the five main continents of the world

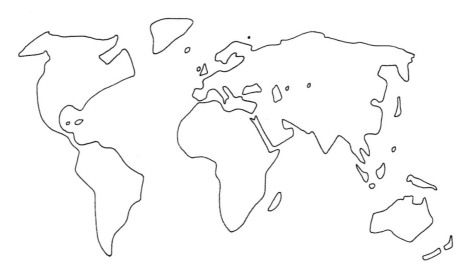

Figure 9.2: An outline map of the world

8 Draw a map of Britain and Ireland as two triangles. Then draw more details to make a more realistic map.

This technique can be used for maps of towns – where squares are more likely building blocks than triangles – or for individual buildings. It is most useful, however, for diagrams. The following diagram of the heart is realistic, but already somewhat simplified. However, it fails completely to demonstrate exactly how the heart functions. The next diagram, which is more schematic, succeeds in turning the heart–lung system into a much more obvious set of processes

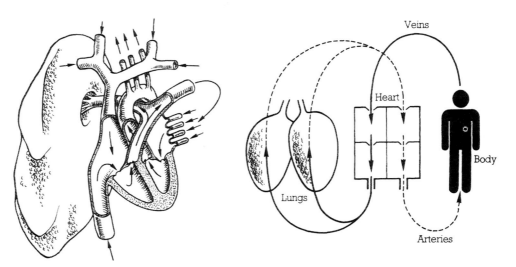

Figure 10: The heart–lung system – realistic and schematic

Note: Activities 9 to 13 in this unit invite you to try your hand at recalling and drawing maps and diagrams, and you will need to have half a dozen sheets of unlined paper to hand for this.

Now look at this diagram of an old-fashioned watch. Simplify it by drawing it as eight circles.

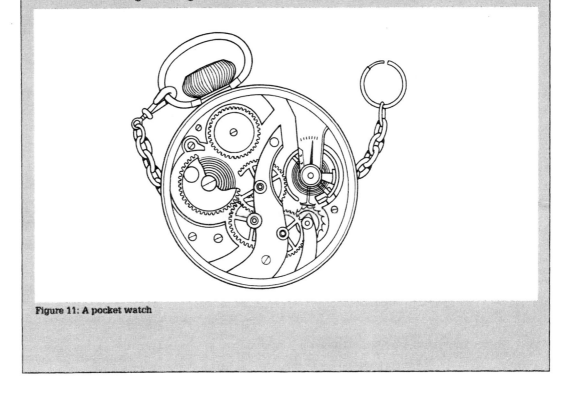

Figure 11: A pocket watch

Your drawing should look something like this:

Figure 12: Circles

The mechanism of the watch may not be obvious, but you have at least begun to understand it, and could redraw it more easily from memory another time if you wished to.

10 Now find a complex diagram or map that represents a process, or a system, or a location that you need to know well. Look for ways in which you can simplify it. Draw a rough sketch of the simplified diagram. Then use the rough sketch to fill in the details of the original diagram. Do this by copying at first, then try again from memory.

The experience of understanding the basic shapes in your diagram – whether circles, squares or triangles – helps you to understand the structure of the whole system much better. You are then in a good position to fill in the details.

22 Shorthand signs for diagrams

Here is a more complicated diagram, taken from Robert Finkel's book *Memory Booster*, which is full of ideas about learning. This example is based on chemistry, but the ideas apply to any kind of diagram – whether of a car engine or the economy of Latvia.

It is a complex idea, but if your are someone who has to draw detailed diagrams, it is worth considering.

Case study 6: Representing amino-acids

Six important amino-acids are called glycine, alanine, valine, leucine, isoleucine, and tyrosine. They all have very different structures from one another, and it is difficult to remember them all. Fortunately, they are composed of only four elements: hydrogen, oxygen, nitrogen and carbon. Even more fortunately, these elements have one, two, three and four electrons respectively and so can be represented like this:

(continued opposite)

H   hydrogen — one atom can link to one other
O   oxygen — one atom can link to two others
N   nitrogen — one atom can link to three others
C   carbon — one atom can link to four others

Fortunately again, amino-acids all contain one particular structure, which can be represented like this:

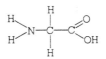

Figure 13.1: Aminoacid

In the case of glycine, the side chain is just one hydrogen atom, so glycine looks like this:

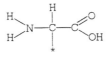

(* is a side chain)

Figure 13.2: Glycine

Thus, the only unique thing about glycine is that its side chain is hydrogen. The rest of the diagram is the same for all amino-acids, so there is no need to copy it over and over again once you have learned it. You can just put it as a box. Glycine is a box with an H below it.

H

Figure 13.3: Glycine simplified

The other amino-acids have more elaborate side-chains, but you can simplify them and still be able to recall all the details. You can put carbon as a full stop and not bother with the H for hydrogen at all. Thus alanine can be simplified in two stages:

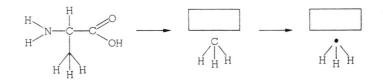

Figure 13.4: Alanine simplified through two stages

Now here are all the rest of the amino-acids in their simplest form:

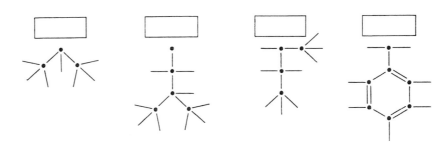

Figure 13.5: Valine, Leucine, Isoleucine and Tyrosine in their simplest forms

These simplified diagrams are easy to reconstitute to the full versions, and easy to remember.

Even if you know no chemistry, you have the clues to replace the box with the original diagram, the full stops with C for carbon, and the empty spaces at the ends of links with H for hydrogen.

It may be completely outside your area of interest, but it is quite exciting to realise that you can rival the experts and draw precise chemical diagrams from memory.

11 Now try drawing the chemical structures of valine, leucine, isoleucine, and tyrosine. You'll find the answer Figure 13.6 at the end of this unit.

This exercise will show you how small, graphically-expressed clues can expand into full-blown, authoritative diagrams. Because you can translate boxes into a basic diagram, much more complex diagrams can be drawn without pausing, as you also translate dots and spaces into carbon and hydrogen.

Action plan

Can you think of any diagrams that you need to draw? Put them in your memory notebook now.

23 Spider charts

The visualisation of abstract ideas has been popularised for twenty years with a layout of notes like the one below, which is based on this unit. These are known variously as mind maps, thought maps, pattern notes or pattern charts. But as they look like spiders, the simplest thing is to call them spider charts.

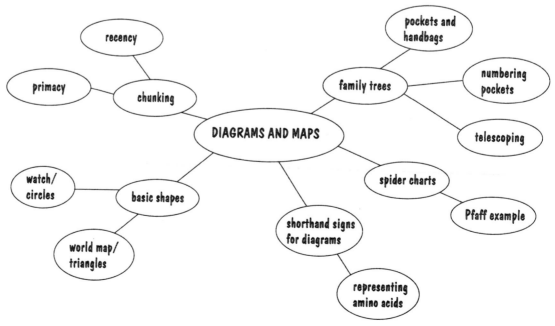

Figure 14: A spider chart

Spider charts are helpful for the same reasons that visual representation is helpful. The charts are:

■ holistic;

■ right-brain oriented;

■ simplified but detailed;

■ memorable because they appeal to your eyes and to your spatial awareness;

■ able to show connections in various, non-linear ways.

They are useful as a means of recording information for yourself and as notes for presenting information to other people. With this technique, you can take notes from a lecture, or make notes from a textbook, or you can assemble ideas in other ways and bring them all together with a spider chart before you write something.

To make sense of – and remember – the meaning of some new information, it is useful to start by creating a spider chart which links together all the main ideas and facts as they come along.

Here is an example from a speech about new industrial sewing machines and their implications for the clothing industry.

It is my firm conviction that we need more training in the clothing industry because the machines they are introducing are becoming more and more complicated.

Consider, for example, the PFAFF range of machines. There are now more than 100 basic models and specific-purpose machines. Some of these are high speed machines and they come with lock-stitch, chain-stitch, single and double needle machines. Some have different feed mechanisms and there is also a bewildering variety of hooks and shuttles.

Mechanised sewing units are now spearheading technological development and these are improving productivity and profits. These units can do everything that the industry requires. They can sew long seams, do dart closing, and make button holes and all at high speed and in mass production. There are also machines which will cater for extra fullness in sleeves and armholes of sackcoats, overcoats and similar garments.

The latest development from PFAFF is the use of mechanised sewing units and integrated sewing stations which set the trend in industrial sewing; no modern factory can afford to be without them. Our industry should be grateful to this company for their exciting range of machines which is helping to make our job easier and our industry more profitable.

The speech is not very well-structured – is it about training, or about machines? – so the first spider chart reflects the chaotic structure.

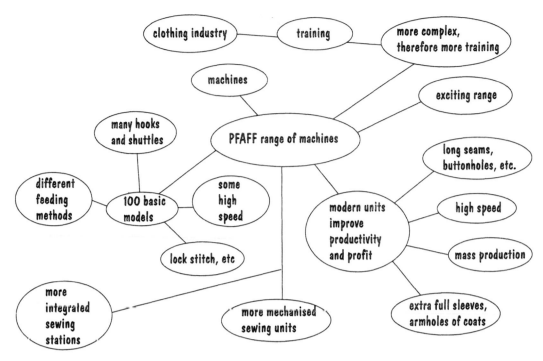

Figure 15.1: First PFAFF spider chart

To make sense of the speech, a new spider chart had to be drawn.

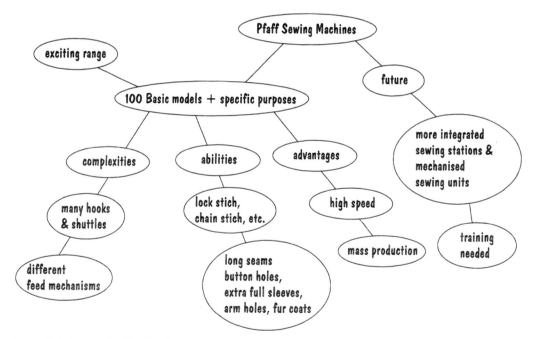

Figure 15.2: Second PFAFF spider chart

From this revised spider chart, it is possible to make conventional notes which encapsulate the meaning of the speech in a logical order – but not in the order that the speech gave it. These notes can now be used to write a report of the speech, or as part of the research for a project on innovations, training or PFAFF products.

PFAFF Sewing Machines

1   Exciting range of 100 basic models and specific purpose machines

   (a) Complexities

      (i)   many hooks and shuttles

      (ii) different feed mechanisms

   (b) Abilities

      (i)   lock stitch, chain stitch, etc.

      (ii) long seams, button holes, full sleeves, armholes for coats

2   PFAFF advantages

   (a) High speed

   (b) Mass production

3   Future prospects

   (a) More integrated sewing stations

   (b) More mechanised sewing units

   (c) Need for more training

1   Find some information that you need to remember; probably a recorded speech or dialogue or a printed text. It should be less than 1,000 words long.

2   Draw a spider chart to summarise its main points. When you have done this, look at the chart and decide whether it needs restructuring. If so, do it.

3   Finally, turn the spider chart into conventional notes with headings, sub-headings, and sub-sub-headings where needed. Lay them out as in the following example.

   heading
     sub-heading
       sub-sub-heading
       sub-sub-heading
     sub-heading
       sub-sub-heading

This way you use the whole width of the page to show how the ideas fit together.

For revision later, the conventional notes are usually more accessible than the spider chart, but the drawing, writing and sometimes rewriting of the chart also help to engage your mind with the material.

If you feel that with the new strength of your memory, you shouldn't need to take notes, then listen to Shakespeare's advice in Sonnet 77:

> Look, what thy memory cannot contain,
> Commit to these waste blanks [*blank pages in a book*], and thou shalt find
> Those children nursed, delivered from the brain,
> To take a new acquaintance of thy mind.

In other words, if you can't remember it, write it down. Your written notes (the children of your brain) will come back and say hello to it later.

Summary

You have now reached the end of Unit 7, and have had the chance to:

➜ organise your memories into snapshot size groups by chunking;

➜ use family trees to make memories within memories by telescoping;

➜ use the same ideas help you remember diagrams with the help of basic shapes and shorthand signs;

➜ use spider charts to help you remember ideas and organise them effectively.

Self-check

This has been a long unit, with 12 challenging activities. Can you remember the names of the techniques you have practised in this unit?

19	F ....
20	N ....
21	T ....
22	B ....
23	S ....

If you need to look up the answers, try backwards chaining and the other re-activating techniques from Unit 2 before you look back through this chapter. And remember to have a look at your memory audit again.

Answers

Activity 1

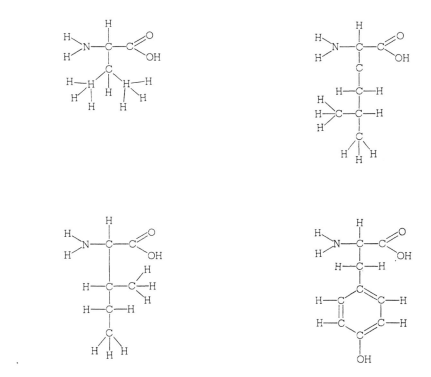

Figure 13.6: The chemical structures of Valine, Leucine, Isoleucine and Tyrosine

UNIT
8

VISIONS

What this unit is about

In this unit we bring together some of the advantages and disadvantages of the visual techniques presented in other units, and ask you to choose a system that works well for you.

In this unit, you will come to the *Memory palace*, perhaps the most flexible and powerful technique in *How to Improve Your Memory*. With your own memory palace you can build up your own unique structure to organise, store and retrieve your memories.

This unit will help you to:

➜ understand the benefits and drawbacks of free visual association;

➜ remember names and faces by association;

➜ build a memory palace to organise your memory beyond the 'rule of seven'.

Visual Association

> There is a power of association. The lyre may recall the player of the lyre, and equal pieces of wood or stone may be associated with the higher notion of absolute equality.

> Plato, *Phaedrus*

Of all the five senses, sight is the most useful for memory. It is said that seeing is believing, but often, seeing is remembering, as well.

You can remember lists associated with humorous scenarios and SMASHING SCOPE, or you can remember numbers by associating them with ostriches, crocodiles and toucans. You can also remember names by making up funny numbers that remind you of the items.

Visual association works both ways – pictures can remind you of words and ideas, and words and ideas can remind you of pictures.

The sorts of associations used above for the Latin names of birds can also be used to remember the names of people you have met.

Case study 5: The Bird-watcher

As a new bird-watcher, I was very proud of all the birds I saw this year; but their names and shapes and habits are new to me, so I've had to use memory tricks to stick them in my mind. The left-hand column shows the picture I've been recalling to keep the birds vivid in their settings, and the right-hand column shows the silly images I used to remember their Latin names.

(continued opposite)

The first one is a tiny bird with a long tail that lives by the water and skims over it, dipping its head below the surface. It's called a dipper (*cinclus cinclus*).

It's a **sink**less, **sink**less. It never **sink**s.

The next one's huge, with a big booming call, and lives by lakes and estuaries. It's a bittern (*botaurus stellaris*).

Bitterns have big **bot**toms and **taurus** is their **stellaris** sign.

Then when I was in the Hebrides I saw a curlew (*numenius arquata*), with its long curved beak, flying over the fields that were shining in the evening sun between the loch and the sea.

It's a **numinous**, holy bird, shining, and it's not **arquat**ic, but lives near water.

I also saw a heron on the loch, standing so still it was hard to see. Its Latin name is *ardea cinerea*.

It's **hardea** to see among the **cinerea** (scenery).

There were a few kestrels, too, *falco tinunculus*, motionless above roads or mountains.

This reminds me of the Maltese **Falco**n, made of **tin**, which I saw with my **uncl**e.

There were lapwings all over the island – *vanellus vanellus*.

It rises and drops like the music of **Vangellis**, **Vangellis**.

I've seen plenty of magpies too, *pica pica*.

Magpies **pica pica** at bright things with their beaks

When I was in Hungary, I saw some storks, white storks. One flew down to another on a nest on a chimney, and they clashed their bills together with a metallic sort of sound. The white stork is *ciconia ciconia*.

Better carry an umbrella near the chimney in case the drunken stork is **ciconia**, **ciconia**.

Finally, there was a wren in a hedge, hiding under a leaf. The wren is *troglodytes troglodytes*.

Tiny cave-dwelling **troglodytes** far from the human world.

1 Have you ever tried to remember an obscure word or name by remembering a visual image associated with it? If so, and if you can remember it, note it here:

24 **Visual Names**

If you want to remember some names, a good way to start is to repeat the names aloud, as suggested in Unit 4 (see page 36). But you can also find images in the names which you can link in your imagination to the memories of the faces. For example, if you meet a bearded man called Chris, you can imagine him with a red hood as Father Christmas. But beware of false associations. An easy mistake was made by the patient whose doctor had the name of a northern city beginning with H, so he addressed Dr Halifax as Dr Huddersfield. If you remember Mr Perch by a fish on his head, be careful not to call him Shark.

2 Look up the names of two or three people whose names you want to remember. Can you think of any visual associations? Note them down below:

The power of images is all right as long as you can control it, but because of unwanted associations, we can all turn Halifaxes into Huddersfields. This is the downside of free visual association, and a reason why a system of set images such as the number-shape pegs can be more helpful in the long-term than all the absurd links of a shopping list or bird list.

Will it be more helpful to you to remember lists with free visual association or with a system of set images? Your choice may be for free association, because it gives the imagination unlimited opportunities for vivid, sensual, humorous and organised fantasies. On the other hand, if you opt for a set system it will require more effort to put in place, but once it is there for you it is more precise.

It is, however, possible to use a technique that combines the advantages of free association with those of set systems, with a memory palace.

25 **Memory palace**

A memory palace is a special place where you put important things you need to memorise. It may be based on a real place, or you can imagine it from scratch. The purpose of it is to provide a memorable structure in which you can imagine the items you need to remember. So, if you have an important shopping list but no paper or pen, as in the case study in Unit 4, you don't have to make up a whole story about can-openers fighting dental floss on tomatoes. Instead, you can just imagine putting each item you want to buy in a different room in your palace.

If your palace is a normal two-bedroom house, and you have a shopping list of eight items, you could put one in each room. Tent pegs could be all over the hall floor, tomatoes could be piled on the mantelpiece in the lounge, a tin-opener could be stuck in the dining room table, dental floss could be draped round the kitchen, margarine could be smeared all over the bathroom mirror, a sharp knife could be quivering in the hatch to the loft, a huge toothpaste tube could be tucked up in the main bedroom, and a tea towel could replace – somewhat inadequately – the curtain in the spare bedroom. The images are startling because you want them to be memorable, but they are also under control because they are kept within the confines of the house.

Your memory palace can be full of throne rooms, galleries and spiral staircases if you want it to be, but equally it can be simple and practical. It can even be one room that you know very well – your bedroom, perhaps. The important thing is that whatever kind of palace you have – a skyscraper or a telephone box – it must feel solid, be well visualised and, most importantly, have plenty of places in it where you can lodge mentally the things you have to remember.

For example, let's suppose I want to make that speech about new sewing machines, and my memory palace is the chamber of the House of Commons. I imagine...

I am standing on the floor of the House, facing the speaker. My main theme is a banner hanging over the speaker's chair saying 'Pfaff'. Higher up, in the press gallery, I see a basic model sewing machine and a specific purpose sewing machine, which has a giant mechanical arm. On their left, I see machines charging up and down the public gallery, being very productive.

My view goes down to the back benches opposite. I can see the MPs with lock stitches, chain stitches, long seams, and armholes in their clothes. On the front bench, the members of the Cabinet have hundreds of hooks, shuttles and feed mechanisms to keep them busy.

Finally, descending from the ceiling on a golden throne comes the future: a mechanised sewing unit with an integrated sewing station attached, and an earnest tutor training them to mass production.

3 How many of the items in this fantasy were cues for the speech? For example, the first cue was the banner saying 'Pfaff'.

You could have counted up to fourteen items in the House of Commons that are cues for the speech.

In this way, the main points of the speech can be remembered quite quickly, and you can speak for some time with no notes. You can use actual objects, or objects that suggest ideas. The idea of training was represented by a tutor, the idea of productivity by fast-producing machines.

You can ensure that you remember all the parts of the speech in the correct order by looking around mentally or walking through your memory palace in a particular sequence. In the House of Commons 'Pfaff' example, the view is of the Speaker's Chair, up to the press gallery, left to the public gallery, down to the back benches, down to the front benches, and then around the whole chamber for the final view of a descending throne.

Your memory palace need not be a big room, as we said before. You could put all the sewing machines and other items in a small room, if you were to shrink them down to, say, the size of a rabbit. You are in complete control.

If you choose to have a memory palace in one room, you can use all the furniture to create visual associations with your theme.

The two case studies below have a one-room memory palace and a large twenty-one-room building respectively. Read them both before you decide whether to make your own memory palace, and what kind of palace it will be.

Case study 6: The extinction of dinosaurs

I wanted to use a very ordinary room for my memory palace; then the contrast would be funny when some very extraordinary things happened in it. I had to learn the theories that account for the extinction of the dinosaurs. This table shows how the dinosaur theory on the left is matched by a memory palace event on the right.

Extinction of dinosaurs	Room
Dinosaurs survived 150 million years, but were extinct by 64 million years ago.	Door with '150 yes', '64 no' on it.
No-one knows why.	Bedside lamp has question marks radiating from it.
Some say it was an asteroid.	Big meteor crashes through the window.
Some say it was volcanoes.	Volcano makes bedclothes erupt.
Another idea, used in Disney's *Fantasia*, was that the sea dried up.	Wardrobe door opens, waves gush out stranding fish on floor, with Mickey Mouse caps.

This series of events in my memory palace gave me a good grounding in dinosaur ideas.

The following Case study is based on the list of people's names remembered in Case study 2 in Unit 4, the story of Aldan Allen and the huge hooker.

Case study 7: Putting faces to names

I was pleased I remembered the whole group of nineteen names from Aldan to Young, but I wanted to do better, and match their faces to their names. So, during our first evening together, I used everybody's name as much as possible, and got to match about half the names with the faces. Then I went through the list by myself later, and from clues like who was with who, what they talked about, what they wore and where they came from, I was fairly sure I had everybody covered. But I had to do a lot of work to memorise them.

My memory palace is my workplace, a four-storey Victorian building with nineteen rooms, which happened to be just the number of people in the group. So I imagined them each in a different room, doing something funny or characteristic of the room. They were in alphabetical order from the basement to the top floor, and some had name badges on to remind me who they were. This is how I visualised them.

(continued opposite)

- Brian Aldan is helping with the post in room 1
- Elizabeth Allen is finding some envelopes in room 2
- Margo Carter is looking up student records in room 3
- Richard Coe is photocopying in room 4
- Audrey Comfort is looking at tutor forms in room 5
- Ivan Fern is reading press cuttings in room 6
- Les Godman is putting plants in accounts, room 7
- Mary Hirons is checking a typist's work in room 8
- Jean Hooker is selling office furniture to the director in room 9
- Pat Hughes is designing a new computer system in room 10
- Barbara Hutchcroft is having lunch in room 11
- Hilary Hutcheson is looking at a horsy book in room 12
- Tony Hutchings is answering the phone in room 13
- Leroy Oliver is checking a new leaflet in room 14
- Barbara Parfitt is checking a balance sheet in room 15
- Carol Phipps is giving me a pay rise in room 16
- Tad Thornhill is describing hang-gliding in room 17
- Andrew Whitehall is being told off in Spanish outside room 18
- Sue Young is writing poetry in room 19.

The following morning, I could put a name to every face I met, at least after a moment's hesitation, while I visualised where they were in my memory palace. My feat of memory helped the atmosphere a great deal.

Some people call a memory palace a 'loci' system, after the plural form of the Latin 'locus' meaning place. Cicero, the most famous Latin orator, used the Senate House in Rome as his memory palace, visualising the images he used to cue the points in his speeches among the columns of the Senate House, up on the ceiling, or on the floor. Similar techniques are found in India and China.

The memory palace is an established, traditional technique. Try it out for yourself now. The process of creating the palace is fun, and you may well find it answers many problems.

4 Design your own memory palace. Draw the floor plan, and the position of any fixed furniture. If it's a real place, spend some time there and observe it carefully. Then, whether it's real or not, close your eyes and, in great detail, imagine yourself looking at everything in your palace. Doors, ceilings, walls, floors, hall, stairs, windows, fittings, furniture. Make it come alive, and practise wandering around it in different directions, inside and out. Look at it from above, sideways and below. Don't put any of its temporary furniture – the items you want to remember from time to time – in it yet. Just concentrate on making the palace itself become brilliantly visible to your mind's eye.

Imagine that you are taking prospective buyers around your memory palace. Talk to the buyers as if you are selling it to them. You could be acting as yourself, or as an estate agent. Describe the palace in glowing terms. Write down your very positive description here:

(continued overleaf)

How is it so far? Is it clear in your mind? Do you like it?

When the palace is clear in your mind, try putting a few cue items in it. If you have nothing else in mind, use the Pfaff sewing machine notes. Put each cue carefully in a specific place, in a particular order. Make sure everything is clearly visible.

When everything is ready, wander mentally through your palace, making a speech about your chosen theme as you wander.

When you try out your palace, you may find weaknesses in it. For example, you may wish you had more places to put things on. But avoid changing it. It takes a lot of effort to dream up a memory palace, and a lot of effort to maintain it solidly in your mind so that it can take a heavy load of memory cues.

You may have noticed that in the 'Pfaff' example in the House of Commons, there were fourteen cue items, and in Case study 6, the memory palace allowed the memorisation of nineteen faces and names – although admittedly some were already familiar. The memory palace, if imagined strongly enough with all the cues in place, can break the rules of primacy, chunking and recency. You can remember more than seven things, and you don't necessarily remember the first and last better than the middle ones. The features of your memory palace should be strong enough to support a large number of memory cues. Properly used and developed, your memory palace can be a highly sophisticated memory device.

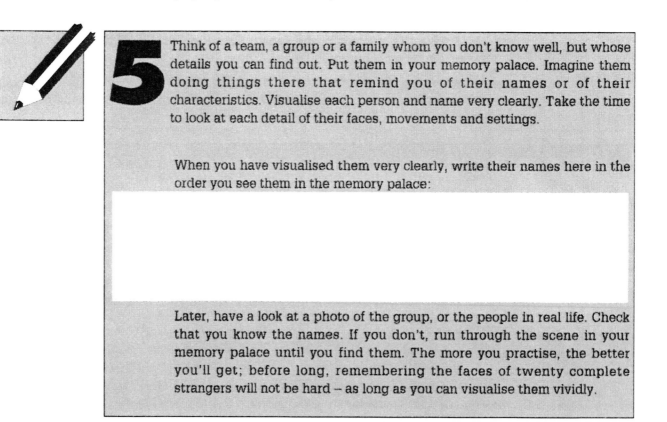

5 Think of a team, a group or a family whom you don't know well, but whose details you can find out. Put them in your memory palace. Imagine them doing things there that remind you of their names or of their characteristics. Visualise each person and name very clearly. Take the time to look at each detail of their faces, movements and settings.

When you have visualised them very clearly, write their names here in the order you see them in the memory palace:

Later, have a look at a photo of the group, or the people in real life. Check that you know the names. If you don't, run through the scene in your memory palace until you find them. The more you practise, the better you'll get; before long, remembering the faces of twenty complete strangers will not be hard – as long as you can visualise them vividly.

Summary

This unit has given you the chance to:

→ consider the benefits and drawbacks of free visual association;

→ remember names and faces by association;

→ build a memory palace to organise your memory beyond the 'rule of seven'.

Self-check

Pause before going on to Unit 9 and ask yourself:

1 How many rooms are there in your memory palace?

2 Why did you choose that size?

3 Can you explain how you chose its general features?

4 What other technique is in this unit?

REVIEW

What this unit is about

So far we have looked at a number of techniques for helping you to remember things, and suggested a number of possible applications for those techniques. Now it's time to review the techniques and make a summary of how they match your needs.

This unit will take you through the techniques that are important to you, you can confirm that they are important by checking your memory of them and your use of them in the book. Then you will have an opportunity to reflect on your experience of working through *How to Improve Your Memory*, and to make a final list of techniques that you intend to apply to areas of your life.

This unit will help you to:

→ recap on the memory techniques;

→ match techniques with your needs;

→ check applications for your techniques;

→ produce a final top ten techniques.

Name your techniques

A good way to make a basic check on whether you will find any technique useful is to see if you remember its name. If you don't remember its name, you may well have decided you don't like the technique.

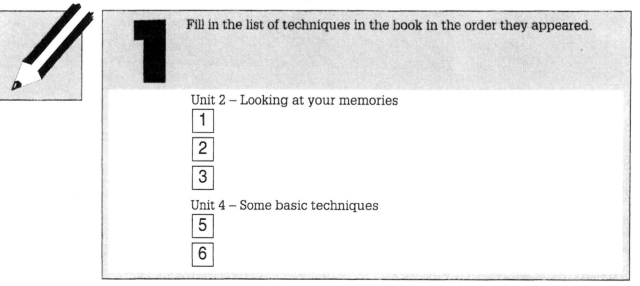

1 Fill in the list of techniques in the book in the order they appeared.

Unit 2 – Looking at your memories

1

2

3

Unit 4 – Some basic techniques

5

6

(continued opposite)

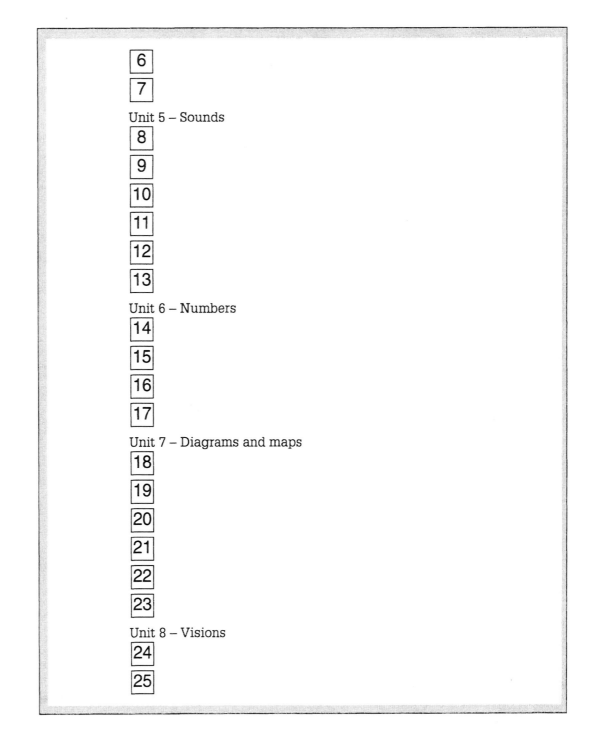

6

7

Unit 5 – Sounds

8

9

10

11

12

13

Unit 6 – Numbers

14

15

16

17

Unit 7 – Diagrams and maps

18

19

20

21

22

23

Unit 8 – Visions

24

25

Here are the answers:

UNIT 2 – LOOKING AT YOUR MEMORIES

  1 Backwards chaining ....

  2 Changing points of view ....

  3 Picking up on pathways and images ....

UNIT 4 – SOME BASIC TECHNIQUES

  4 Physical memory aids ....

  5 Initial-letter words ....

  6 Initial-letter sentences ....

  7 Funny stories ....

UNIT 5 – SOUNDS

  8 Repeating names ....

  9 Initial letter alliteration ....

 10 Verse and worse ....

 11 Word shapes (right brain) ....

 12 Spotting rules (left brain) ....

 13 Read/copy/hide/write ....

UNIT 6 – NUMBERS

 14 Funny Numbers (to remember other things) ....

 15 Sentences for numbers ....

 16 Number shapes ....

 17 Funny formulae ....

UNIT 7 – DIAGRAMS AND MAPS

 18 Family trees ....

 19 Numbering pockets ....

 20 Telescoping ....

 21 Basic shapes ....

 22 Shorthand signs for diagrams ....

 23 Spider charts ....

UNIT 8 – VISIONS

 24 Visual names ....

 25 Memory palace ....

If there are techniques which you forgot but which you really want to use, add them to the list above.

Use your techniques

As a second check of the techniques that are really useful to you, look down this list of the things that you memorised, so as to practise the techniques. Tick the items that you think you remember.

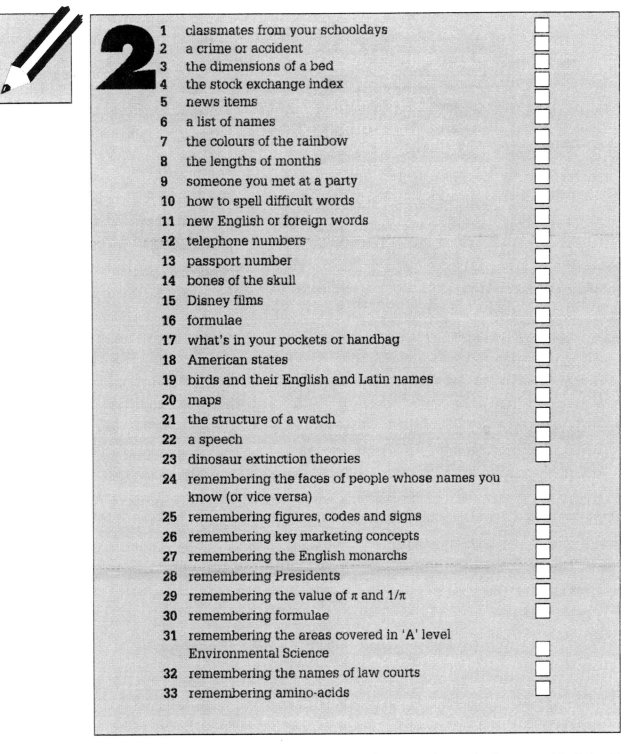

1 classmates from your schooldays
2 a crime or accident
3 the dimensions of a bed
4 the stock exchange index
5 news items
6 a list of names
7 the colours of the rainbow
8 the lengths of months
9 someone you met at a party
10 how to spell difficult words
11 new English or foreign words
12 telephone numbers
13 passport number
14 bones of the skull
15 Disney films
16 formulae
17 what's in your pockets or handbag
18 American states
19 birds and their English and Latin names
20 maps
21 the structure of a watch
22 a speech
23 dinosaur extinction theories
24 remembering the faces of people whose names you know (or vice versa)
25 remembering figures, codes and signs
26 remembering key marketing concepts
27 remembering the English monarchs
28 remembering Presidents
29 remembering the value of π and $1/\pi$
30 remembering formulae
31 remembering the areas covered in 'A' level Environmental Science
32 remembering the names of law courts
33 remembering amino-acids

How many of these did you really memorise? Answer honestly, because this list will affect your choice of techniques for future use.

Identify your techniques

3 The list below shows which techniques you practised in order to remember all the items you ticked above. For every item in the list that you ticked, check on the key below whether the technique is one that you wish to use.

The techniques we used to remember all these items were:

1 backchaining, changing points of view, picking up on pathways and images

2 as **1**

3,4 number-shape technique

5 your choice

6 funny story, repeating names, verse, funny numbers, number-sound/shapes, family trees, telescoping, visual names, memory palace

7 initial letter sentence

8 verse

9 repeating names, visual names

10 word shapes, spot rules, read/copy/hide/write

11 as **10**

12 number-sound pegs, words for numbers

13 number-sound pegs

14 funny numbers

15 funny numbers

16 funny numbers, number-sound pegs

17 counting pockets, chunking

18 family trees

19 visual names

20 basic shapes

21 basic shapes and shorthand signs

22 memory palace, spider charts

23 memory palace

24 memory palace, visual names

25 number-shape pegs

26 initial-letter alliteration

27 verse

28 verse, family trees

29 words for numbers

30 number-shape pegs

31 funny numbers

32 funny numbers

33 shorthand signs

How many useful techniques can you now identify?

Retain your old techniques

Now think about the techniques you already used before you started this book – and perhaps used in the first activity – on a news item from yesterday. Do you have confidence in your old techniques? Are they a part of your everyday routine? If so, you should stick with them. For example, you may very happily use a diary for appointments. As a result, you may have no desire to replace your diary with a new technique.

In your Memory Notebook you may well have included a wide range of things to memorise, and a number of alternative techniques for many of them. Look back at your list of priority techniques now, and adjust your priorities if necessary. You might have thought that, say, the number-shape peg system was a low priority, but then put it against several examples in the list of things you remembered. So you might want to give it a higher priority, or you might want to look for other techniques touse to memorise the same example.

Your top ten techniques

To settle your choice of preferred techniques, write here up to ten techniques that you intend to use:

Reflection

Well, that gives up to ten resolutions on memory – good intentions at least. The problem now is to build these techniques into your everyday life, both your studying and your other time. Only when you are using the techniques confidently, and as part of your general repertoire of skills, can you say that you have fully taken them on board. That will only happen when you see evidence that the techniques work for you in practical situations, not just in this book.

How do you feel after all this work on improving your memories? Has it been depressing, exhilarating, or just as you might have predicted?

The more effort you put into memorising, the more you will remember. That is how it should be, as in Ebbinghaus's remorseless experiments. But your effort should also reap real successes, and should encourage you to put similar effort into other memorising techniques in future.

Why not look back now at some of the activities that you have done in the book. Look particularly at the ones where you feel that you did not remember well, and try to work out why you didn't remember. Was it a matter of too little interest, or too much anxiety? Not enough motivation, or not enough effort? Perhaps the task was too hard?

Another reason for forgetting could have been that your pacing was wrong. The learning spiral on page 27 showed you how to learn for short periods, have frequent breaks, and go back to an item at longer and longer intervals to make sure you still recall it. Was the pacing a problem with your elusive memory?

If any of these questions get a sure 'yes', then the activities don't throw much light on the effectiveness of the memory techniques as such.

The effectiveness of the memory activities will be influenced by your general motivation and attitude – which is perfectly natural. There is no reason to force yourself to do something which does not interest you. There are plenty of ways to improve your memory, and even if just one technique in this book has helped you, that will have made the effort worthwhile.

You will probably find that, if you compare notes with another user of this book, you will have completely different lists of what works best for you. Activities are always easier for some people than others, and certain types of memorising appeal to certain types of people. This is because we all have different learning styles, as we saw in Unit 1.

Remember, however, that *active* learning is effective learning. You may like traditional learning styles with a tutor and a textbook, or groupwork, or computer-assisted learning, or research projects. Whatever your preference, you will be able to make any kind of learning active and involving through your knowledge of how memory works and your choice of memory techniques, as a result of the ideas in this book,.

So, in a sense, we have come full circle. You are an individual with your own learning style. You should find these ideas about memory that you have read very helpful. It is up to you now.

Summary

In this unit you have:

➜   recapped on the memory aids and techniques;

➜   matched techniques with your needs;

➜   checked applications for your techniques.

You have to have the will to succeed, the right frame of mind, and the times and rhythms for good study. Then, the memory techniques you have chosen will come into their own. Learning will always involve effort, but now the effort can be more productive, and more fun.

APPENDIX

READING LIST

Most general references to 'researchers' or 'research' in the text and some of the memory techniques and examples come from:

Cohen, G. *Memory – Current Issues*, 2nd edn, Open University Press, 1993

Baddeley, A. *Your Memory – A User's Guide*, Penguin Books, 1992

Long-term memory retention evidence is given in:

Cohen, G. *The Psychologist*, 1992

The 'forest model' of memory is based on the model in:

Rose, S. *The Making of Memory*, Bantam Press, 1992,

which also gave most of the thoughts on misleading ideas of the past.

'SMASHING SCOPE' as an acronym for underpinning ideas appears in:

Buzan, T. *Use Your Memory*, BBC Books, 1983

The ideas behind telescope thinking, the amino-acids diagrams and the dinosaur theory example of a memory palace are all taken from:

Finkel, R. *Memory Booster*, Piatkus, 1993

Acknowledgements

Thank you to Ros Morpeth, Denman College, Tim Burton, Trevor Weston, Professors Roger Lewis, Gillian Cohen and Steven Rose, Christine von Rabenau, Lorna Rogers and especially Sonia Leach.